PARADISE, LATER YEARS

Caitlin Press Inc.
8100 Alderwood Road,
Halfmoon Bay, BC V0N 1Y1
www.caitlin-press.com

Text and cover design by Vici Johnstone.
Printed in Canada

Caitlin Press Inc. acknowledges financial support from the Government of Canada
and the Canada Council for the Arts, and the Province of British Columbia through
the British Columbia Arts Council and the Book Publisher's Tax Credit.
Library and Archives Canada Cataloguing in Publication

Quednau, Marion, author
        Paradise, later years / Marion Quednau.

Poems.
ISBN 978-1-987915-83-9 (softcover)

        I. Title.

PS8583.U337P37 2018   C811'.54   C2018-903538-2

Paradise, Later Years

Marion Quednau

Caitlin Press, 2018

In memory of my mother

*and for all the women
of December*

Tell the ones you love, you
love them;
tell them now.
—*Dennis Lee*

I can't come back. I won't change.
I have the usual capacity for wanting
what may not even exist…
—*Galway Kinnell*

Contents

HOLIDAY

Sent to the Moon

You won't get far
dressed like the Queen of Sheba, chasing after
the sun and the moon—
                        Slant advice
as you slammed the door, so crazy-brave
in your scrap of miniskirt and kick-ass cowboy boots, halter of Thai silk
            crossing your heart, and you hoping not to die.
                        What Queen? What Sheba?
You wanted only
                        the world, wanted to feel
the dark heat of family tether
                        come undone. Now you see

how you were sent to the moon, its shiny device
        as bait, or blessing—
                        and how far you've come, giving
to restored habitat for panda, and the unsheltered
among us, earth-shaken Guatemalans in their endless *temblores,*
the orphans of Sri Lanka after the tsunami's wild wet,
then Haiti, always a coup or clashing of wills—
your gazebo aflutter with faded prayer flags from Tibet.
        And recycling; let's face it, there's too much stuff.
The white rocker boots, sharp-toed
in your cache of sorry lovers' belongings;
                        you always wanted to be the one
betrayed, blameless,
            not calling it quits,
ditched the faux soldier garb of Army & Navy,
        the greatcoats and gritty shirts with epaulettes,
all the high-fidelity woofers and tweeters, garden Buddhas
        that came after the Beatles,
and didn't feel much
                        remorse. So now imagine
it had been otherwise. Think of the stone chip in your windshield
        as a star, no less beautiful

for you once conceiving it as bad luck. Pretend
the man ahead in the souped-up Buick Skylark
            is a receiver of gifts, despite
his greyed shag and wary glances over his shoulder—
        he probably smokes, too—but imagine
you have long travelled in cahoots, unconsoled,
are newly sending signals
                    of sweet recognition, hearts torn
amid the broken contours of strip mall and suburb. Suppose
one wintered marriage had been enough—
        ritual dance in the bedclothes, and urging
of children as fine measure
                    for providence. Imagine

        that the news from East Timor—
or anywhere, once Burma or Bosnia, Rwanda, flamed-out
            New York and then, oh God, for years, Iraq—
had been dispatches of love. Dust hills of Afghanistan
returned to verdant green, machetes of Africa become
soft vessels carrying water to the mouth.
        Know the grace notes
playing in your ear late nights on *Radio Netherlands*—
            believe in
trembling flocks of birds lost in migration
still finding a hard-wired jog home,
        every pressed species, even our own young
addicts and hackers, avid bankers, returned
to good ground. All that rushing
to circumnavigate, plant a flag, like Champlain
        or that sorry dog sent in virtual pursuit
of the moon, and panting to death, purple-tongued—
you long for greater invention
        beyond fresh latitudes of fear
and piracy, the seas moaning with hankering
        for human cargo, shark-fin soup.
                    You want something

like a giant flipped coin—bright whimsy,
                    heads-or-tails, perfect catch—
as you reach land's end, park by the darkened Pacific,
hear in its mantra of wave after dashed wave
        that you are still smart, and young,
                    with nothing but second chances,
so you give it a shot, send acronyms into satellite heavens
        riven by archers and angry gods,
the earth's shadow
        dolled up as dark sun on a moonwalk:
OMG SWEET ECLIPSE, WHERE RU? XOLOL
The answer's not long in coming—
        love pinged off a tower, nobody home—
a see-sawing of stars, electric scrimshaw in your bones,
no ring tone but the rising wind.
        Your mother has requested a meeting
in the hereafter, and your father's still
digressing, has his good days—and bad.
                    Your heart riots, you can't accept

the upshot, how everything comes apart,
broken and in ruins—
                    and still remains the same.
You strive for sleep as entrance to the world,
        find a small blue door
among the barren highlands of what once was, thin goats
        gleaning the spoils of chastened continents,
children with machine guns
                    brokering deals of safe passage.
You have to walk
        to re-enter the old places, there's no other way.
At first light it begins, the brimming and shudder
        of what's missing, what belongs.
                            A bridge,
sky-scraped city, street grifter
        shucking quarters from passersby—he howls
of salvation, how it's unforgiving,

this turning back
            to goodness, and too damned slow.
He wants proof

        that you're cleaning up your act;
you're not in a hurry, too proud
                to drop to your knees
beside him and join the noise, holler along,
                    you can't tell if it's praise or blame,
you're making it up as you go, feeling
the raw edges of everything, time
                and its pilfering, you're on a roll
with this one-man plainsong pop-up band,
                your canting off-key, off-kilter
but no one seems to mind, a few blank faces
on their shunting way to work, stopping
                        to listen up,
their loosened smiles raining down
                    like small change—

Penguins

When the first-grade teacher told jokes on Friday afternoons—the children about to be released—he wanted to ease the disappointments ahead. The weekend would be full of mistakes, some more glorious than others, he seemed to be saying.

What do penguins eat for breakfast? he asked, the backpack-ridden youngsters in a rapt circle at his feet. They were intent, with their heated faces and raised hands, on being remarkable, not mere specks on the ancient blue globe in the classroom, its spinning bent out of shape by someone knocking it about.

Ice Krispies, he said. Hilarious to six-year-olds, who haw-hawed with zeal. *Next week you can bring something funny to share, a story—or riddle, knock, knock*—rapping his knuckles on his greying noggin for effect.

I could see, from the doorway, what he was up to. He held clout, would be heard in the months to come, when he spoke of numbers and letters. The precision required. So, a ruse perhaps. Self-saving persona. But it was more—he wanted to be inside their heads when these innocents thought of ice, or spilled cereal, missed their marks. Wanted to give reassurance, be remembered—and feel the returns of love.

How about when somebody pees his pants? a sniggering boy asked, trying to upset the natural order of teacher, funny, kids laughing. *You know what would be even sillier*—the tall, stooping pundit offered, bending like the willow in a Basho haiku—*if someone* almost *peed his pants, now that would be a hoot.*

Genius. No upbraiding the kid, and the gist of it, no one gets hurt. Almost died laughing, almost got married, almost hit black ice, almost ignored that teensy red spot on a worried brow and whoops-a-daisy, almost got cancer. He was setting these kids straight about the fine line between paid attention and "never saw it coming." That we're all to blame for our own precious slip-ups, and can often—but not always—save ourselves.

You're almost dismissed, he said, with a wry smile, when the bell rang and not one child moved.

Long Weekend

                                Each time I was shocked
by the cold, dull sensation
                    of exacted sacrifice—
house-spoiled tabby mown down while hunting like a novice
along the highway's verge, splayed possum with its delicate pink tail
and broken-backed doe, dithering at the centre line,
trying to rise—
                        the animal faces swept clean of intent,
crows plucking eyes, and clouds of flies feasting at the blackened innards,
the pattern of abundant life once secretive
                        now torn, made plain—
the car's shadow fleeing through the flickering light
                    as we swept across the province, on holiday.

I couldn't stand to look, couldn't look away.
                    My father, in his pointed disregard,
daring me to buck up. Take it all in stride.
                    "What's wrong?" he said in the rear-view mirror,
thump-thumping over some downed beast
so I could feel the price of existence.
                                Merciful, I think he called it.

I'm clear about it now.
                    The time of grace
has ended. Traffic is trespass,
            headlong and tedious, unrelenting
and we complain—kill even our own—haven't a clue
how to stop this rough sport, more than 100,000 horses
disappeared from the streets of American cities—starved or slaughtered—
to make way for the bicycle, and then things got worse.
                        We like to drive, open throttle,
to new-scraped frontiers, the creatures endlessly routed
and there are more of us, more signatures
            of blind collision, more twinned lights
beamed through the helpless

animal brains (and we too possess
    such a heave-ho device, *hippocampus*, high on impulse,
short on regret). There aren't enough
blunted blows with crowbars for compassion
        as we meet the animals, blameless
        and unblaming, red-tailed hawk in mid-dive agony,
raccoon saying its dainty prayers, bear cub mewling
for its struck mother—the cops arriving with guns as if it were a crime
            to simply be alive—
        a lingering last glance of friction in all our eyes.

    These are the effects.
The cause is in our puffed-up species thinking itself
            rare and precious, each one of us
having exclusive right-of-way toward finicky desire;
                    now *that's* heavy traffic.
Made devious by want, even to ourselves,
we are strangely unaccountable—
                    redemption rumoured to exist
at some distance, in the journey itself,
        leaving town and finding love, nothing off limits—
        our suspect heroes behind the wheel, almost getting away
with murder: think Thelma and Louise
singing their last hurrah over the cliff's edge,
            free as caged birds. Sad, but they're happy, right?

Remember taking a Sunday drive,
the whole family piling in, just because we could?
Taking the long route home for the thrill
of crossing the near-washed-out bridge? Well, the whole deal
        of driving ourselves to distraction
is off—we're teasing out the last days of the roving car
as if we might yet
            find intelligent life among the stars,
    diehards placing last bets on the poker-faced moon.

So much simpler
to have thrown open the windows, learned
        the names of the trees
arm's length from the house, *cascara*
often confused with the *alder-leaved buckthorn,*
            its tight-grained softwood once slipping through fresh water
as small dug-out canoe, a bitter drug drawn from the bark
        by the First Peoples in their healing.

    Easier to have pushed
the lonesome child
            calmly on a swing, back and forth,
sharing the stories behind our everyday captures,
        rabbits making ideal first pets—the boy has told you so,
his legs scissored against the sky—their bunny hearts
beating two hundred times a minute, faster on warm days
                or when hard-pressed to jump this way, or that.

    Better to have tangled
in the unmade bed, shown tender preference
for the body lightly napping beside you,
            fumbling and unfastening toward
exacting joy—your small startled gasps—
                    the vanished afternoon made bright
in this sweet coursing of catch-and-release, easing
the stale-mated human conundrum
                of ever wanting more.

        You might have walked
from the wooden shade to broad sunlight,
                marking the slim difference
between yesterday's sullen heat and this morning's
                        rusted scent of foliage;
each year the ready dew of autumn
                catches you by surprise.

After Saturday and Sunday,
those days that released you as a child
beyond the bricked school, where you gratingly learned
        science and human invention,
the touted combustion engine and all finicky numbers
        as small cogs in a bigger wheeling of stars and inklings—
when you touched the fear, bright intersecting
of beauty with loss,
        the window-smacked bird, its frail, frail
bones and feathers when it flew upward
                        from its shocked shadow, recovered
its lightness in the face of your dark-scraped hole
for the tiny, cardboard crypt—
                        you might have believed
there was nothing more needed
        than a sense of direction, the invisible
working of light,
        a nearing of water.

        But there was always nightfall.
The next day. Watching the toad caught by the heavy rains
in the cellar's window well
                        and setting it free. Following it
then in its hippety-hop-hop-hop to a ground cover of dark leaves,
its delicate, righted privacy beyond reach—
you scarcely knew
        where the freighted animals might go,
still wild and abiding
                        between accidents.

Think about it—

                      as a flame-dousing firefighter
who loved me in the off-season
used to say, to get me all hot and bothered;
          he was brash, bent on misbehaving, spent summers
in boot camps with rednecks hanging their girlfriends' bras as faux shrines,
he, who playfully used the word *cherish*
               in describing my love status while chatting up
the pharmacist over a packet of prophylactics,
         so I do, *I think about it,* how much I've saved
in the long run, like some hard-earned high-return desire
retirement plan, in not having a true love
on the Feast Day of St. Valentine,
who literally lost his head—had it nicely lopped off—
               in adoration of God,
the holiday since become a kitsch fest for sweethearts
after Chaucer, in his lusty *Canterbury Tales,*
          noted birds coupling in spring
and Shakespeare's Ophelia, so lovestruck
            as to go staring mad, named herself Hamlet's Valentine:
everyone in modern times still trying
to prove the intangible
             stuff of desire
to be as real as pain, a stab to the heart—
         while we tease out right Cupid-words
to catch another's gaze, lay claim.
         The man I swore would be my last
giving me a single rose
by way of idling white delivery van at half-past six—
                 it's amazing to what lengths a man will go
to be remembered as *smitten* (his sign-off)
              and scared to death:
         a few red petals
and he's off the hook. His telephone too.

Another February, another winsome

suitor become tall, dark stranger;
                      he regrets
our going out, claims the splashy dinner too expensive
for *what it was*—
              clams vongole, lots of slurp and salt,
and me all dolled up like a fast-and-loose flapper
        with my trailing boa, hoping for
a few speak-easy moves on the dance floor, hepped-up
half-jazzy waltz, or even the *Watusi*—
                but he's slurring his martinis,
says he doesn't understand
all the fuss, never does anything especially lovey-dovey
with his wife.
           Gong goes my *Who Wants to Marry a Millionaire*
game-show heart with this cheap trivia,
             and the night's basically mine;
      so I sing a little
back-up karaoke—*na-na-na-na, na-na-na-na, hey hey hey goodbye*
with the local firemen, all savagely good-looking
        and *tant pis,* too young,
but what the sweet fuck, everyone's having fun
          and I hit some hot-mamma notes on "Mustang Sally."

      But seriously, think about it—
no man's sweater with yarned yachts on the chest,
drooping in the sleeves
        where I'd dreamed him longer in reach,
no Lands' End shirt in fake suede, guaranteed to be comfy round the neck
where a skimpy pony tail or hockey player's mullet
declares a man's retro sense of style, and despite
        the colour clearly being swimming-pool blue
the nattily dressed urban cowboy asking, *Is that mauve?*
      I still wonder if he ever knew
my eyes were green, that my dark hair held highlights
          of red, a burnt umber. But no matter;
I'd been counselled from an early age to think
        of the man first, not for the sake of enduring love,

just to keep his attention—on himself.
So I played by the rules, and then I didn't:
                              no high-tech Lee Valley tools
for making something folk-artsy for the man cave,
in this case a coal-oil-smelling Chris-Craft
                              moored under the Burrard Bridge,
or antique captain's chair (some real seaman's ass
having worn the seat to a smooth patina), no
state-of-the-art pool cues
            and never mind that I can beat him at eight ball,
it's *Watch-and-learn, hold the chalk, sister*—
                        No sitting through blam-blam-blam
action movies, where the babe is always treason
and can look forward to a rip-roaring chase scene
                  with the good guy/slash/double spy, bon-cop-on-top
and all of his heroics in the bedroom,
                        no slightly foolish hats, a middle-ager
wearing his revolutionary Che Guevara beret, playing up his pep
                  by driving a sporty MG with a rusty muffler
and despite the cold sleet, putting the top down.
                  John Lennon's dead, remember?

            No explaining what I *would have wanted*—
                              that's a big, fat relief.
I hate last-minute chocolate, it's so passive-
                  aggressive, that lure of soft-centre, hard nougat,
            cinnamon hearts, the lingering mouth burn
                        of the whole red bustier, garter getup
like I'm giving the keynote address to an AGM of men
            who fear commitment, the room empty
'cause they're all on the make for any soft-porn good sport
                        who doesn't talk at all—
            But who's counting?
In my version of swoon and see-you-soon
I would have preferred
            home-grown bouts in the bedclothes,
no drunken debates as warm-up bands to the overrated

main act of macho pelvic sashay,
no shackles or gotch-wearing contests, just a rucked-up
               flannel nighty and being waylaid
on old-fashioned impulse in a dark hallway, midway to the loo,
a soft hand on a cheek, some tenderness
                              tipping the apple cart,
the kind of attention that resolves its own puzzle,
ends where it begins—
                    in a clean, sparked sensation,
my skin so bright and polished
          it might have been placed over my bones
               a rosy hour ago, give or take,
my breathing reclaimed
          as boundless, blameless, I'll never flag or fail,
yes, something so simple and pure,
                    it *is* like riding a bike—
round and round the block, basking in the risk,
the world truly stirred and shaken,
                    the sudden press of light
against every tree's every leaf—the air shimmers—
and I'm ten again, could spend all afternoon
                    just keeping my balance.

          I'm done with pierced hearts, a series
of cad-studded Cupid moments, and this year, in a faltering spring
               uncertain of its own sweet hurry,
I'm taking a walk on the wild side
               with my dog—he's dapper, a real canine Cary Grant
and he gets it, the whole tug-of-war, strength-in-loyalty thing,
          retrieving of loved objects over and over, no regrets,
teasy kisses in my ear while we're driving toward the mountains,
the world brimming after winter's worst:
                    there's a heady patience
in the trifling air, a budding on all the stiff trees.
          So walkies it is, a rude slap of rain in my face
when the wind hustles off the coast
               and then tucking in early;

I could re-watch *Some Like It Hot* with its farce antics
set against the Valentine's Day Chicago gangland massacre,
      that froggy voice of Tony Curtis in drag
and Jack Lemmon as sassy bowlegged girl tippy-toeing in heels,
      or find a good book, the duvet drawn up
to my still-not-half-bad breasts, my stoppered-up heart
almost forgotten
              in the sway of story, an unreliable narrator
spilling his guts while stuck in some aggrieved
                war or childhood, and I put up with him
talking his way into the wee hours,
his shy mix of flaws, hair always in his eyes,
      and maybe he dies at the end—or maybe not—
when out of the blue of near-dawn, it's that late,
      the phone rings.

             And I have to *think about it,* who in the hell
it might be, oh, the single-rose fellow
      taking a stab at belated real-time emotion
(he's always had that breathless, boy-on-the-run voice):
"I would have married you!"
      he spouts, as if that's a good thing,
like a crashed pilot
      swearing he could have pulled it off, flying blind
through the passes, if only, if only,
      he'd seen the steep mountains ahead.
"Stop shouting," I whisper, as if there might yet be
            an aching lover beside me, "I believe you."
And then silence, the line gone dead
while I'm inwardly celebrating
      our tenth avowed anniversary, a quiet party
for two, no fanfare or gifts of tin or tourmaline;
we're simply walking, hand in hand,
      through a meadow of bright yellow daffodils,
their heads bobbing
             yes and yes and yes and yes

Sunlight Gleams Briefly from a Harrow in a Field

I.

School's out, and the chase is on
to be *somewhere else*, the packed-up kids and trikes, fretted family dog
all hitting the road—
neat freaks and rote TV-watchers afraid of spiders
suddenly gone gypsy, bare feet stuck out the windows,
faux hunter-gatherers jimmying for position
to find the best campsite, first slack-jawed fish,
and already vexed
by the cyclists teetering along the highway's verge,
gusts of smoke from the wildfires ahead.

It's a gruelling portage,
cities emptied, cars staggered against the mountains
towing land-lubbered boats called *Magpie III* or *Sweet Mary*,
and we're in the thick of it—
four women at loose ends
(unappeased children and lovers
gone their separate ways),
our revamped cutie-pie Airstream crammed
with chi-chi coffee gizmos, collapsible yurt, and trashy bare-bosomed
novels claiming that willful damsels
died of adulterous love
among swarms of mosquitoes, of the blood loss, infection, alleged guilt;
but here we are, with the giddy sense of being owed
an easing of daily imperfections, bright favours
from surrounding nature, our eyes searching
the scorched valley for elusive signs of the serendipitous
moment. The stuff of memories.
Hijinks of rare loyalty
or affection, photographable moments of high-water
comeuppance, our wide smiles of relief
to prove we existed at all.

Hats off to us
we shout, fanning our open shirt fronts—
                    we're all bras and bravado, taking the back roads,
plan to be cowgirls in the Quilchena, collect postcards
from classic ma-and-pa diners and bad motels implausibly called
The Last Resort or The Shady Rest;
                              there's risk on our minds,
we want the narrative raw and decisive, long to be
lost—then found, nicely sunburnt, just off the trail,
                                        struck by the immensity—
          the land seeming to roam almost on its own
against our stunted progress into the ancient trees.
                    We want to *be moved*—
by the sway of the eight-hundred-mile-long river, some grand design,
          nothing close at hand except bugs and wild animals
on the prowl, the spirit world
                    granting the chosen sweet tricks
of transformation;
                    a clutch of women going it alone
might lock eyes at dusk with a who-knows-what,
                         a wolf, or something stranger—
          there's bound to be shape-shifting, a sharp stump rearing up
as feathered bird, the old ruse of spun water,
                    we feel both the pull and the fear—
might just get what we want
                              in surprising new skins.
          Yet it seems a crime
to have this idle time, the want of ourselves,
like the sweet lies of childhood
                    sticking in our throats—
and soon enough, if the humdrum of clammy hours
          mocking sappy songs by Abba is quick music,
                         we are speaking of mothers.

II.

    Scrub-a-dub, dub,
the first says, marvellously offended, even yet,
I was already fifteen, and she'd hover,
clean my bathtub rings—imagine!
        I stopped washing—started
doing drugs. Her guilt trip—my ripping head trip.
        We all laugh, the jagged, nervous sort.
This woman still wears the warm glow of long-drawn baths
and rebellion, is a man magnet,
        the wrong sort, grifters and abusers.
We have to worry about her, we really do.

Eat up, eat up, eat up, the second murmurs
        as bitter incantation, a swoop of hair
like an upside-down fern on her puzzled forehead.
I'd poke through tuna casseroles, pick out
the yucky bits in her famous fucking English trifle;
        I got fed up
with being more deserving than the starving children wherever—
        threw up any chance I could.
Her anger is soft-spoken, still in small mouthfuls.
        The losing of appetite
seems at odds with insatiate youth,
        girls clambering up trees, seeking advantage,
the boys below in the shadows
            playing at becoming unreliable
cops and cowboys, shooting one another,
then failing at dying.
            Death always left us famished.
        The staring eyes, requisite
pomp-and-circumstance of burying the small, stiff bodies,
mostly birds, and once
        a whole bucket of kittens, drowned.
        We vowed never again
to mow that mean person's lawn, all for a few measly bucks.

But we did.
               Childhood was all about betrayal.
Our mouths full of plums, dark watermelon
       seeds, sorted by our tongues,
and sandwiches cut just so, salmon bones and salami rinds
       removed by resolute mothers in frumpish aprons—
who wanted to please us, nothing more.
            We knew only our gaping hunger, not its price.

     Zing, zing, zing with the zippers,
I swear I still hear a phantom Singer sewing machine,
the third offers as bait.
     She's named Coco, after the infamous heiress.
Some God-awful shirt-dress in purple paisley,
         a nip-and-tuck so things hung properly.
I am her progeny, she says, holding her grudge beautifully,
still svelte at fifty-looking-forty, a perfect clothes rack.
          She's driving with gusto to make up lost time;
if we get pulled over, she'll cozy up to the cop—
                get away with it.

III.

     Then it is my turn,
            this bad mouthing of mothers
sweeter with pretend guilt than stopping for ice cream.
     They all look to me, keen for the lack
in my mother's tending. Surprised to be in the pickle she's in,
tilting in high heels toward our aggrieved beck and call.
              And I want to say
she smocked our dress fronts, painstakingly,
brushed the felt of our first store-bought winter coats, pea jackets
she claimed made us look like sailors or gadabouts,
     but that she didn't mind, not really.
Did we dawdle coming home? Or run pell-mell,
stray dogs chasing us as we charged through the door
trying to find her?
         I'm almost sure

she made soup from scratch, she must have,
from a ham bone, with sticky dumplings, and like true ingrates
        we didn't care for its cloying taste.
But there was never an expectation,
                    no certain time or place or plateful.
     Summers, I know for a fact,
she dried us off after swimming, holding the towels around us
on the shore of some shockingly cold lake or other—
                   as though we, the children, were ballast,
already the stronger ones, bound to save her.

                  I want to say
it is a privilege of love—of being loved—
                      to lay blame.
     My mother dying so young
left little legacy of true failings—or forgiveness.
     Sunlight gleams briefly from a harrow in a field,
the river churning with freshet toward the sea a given, irrefutable.
I am careful to make my voice tender,
                 without reproach.
     My mother loved the world too much
to worry. She left us largely alone, free to roam.
                We were trusted—
They jump on me, all three,
     like addled Grade Eight girls in their vented spleen.
No one has a mother like that, they jeer. *Your mother*
             isn't real. You've made her up—
I somehow expected
          they would be green with envy, young and green
        as the first cut of fallen hay—oh, that heavenly scent.

          We fall silent then,
the sunlight as wide as the river is long.
     Ice cream, my treat, I offer
         some miles down the road, outside Hope,

where the faded billboard—a woman in fifties' frock and still undaunted—
leans over the highway.
I'm thinking
double scoop, chocolate sprinkles, cherry on top.

Sundays

Sundays were reminder
                that death was in the air—
       and weren't we the lucky ones to still feel
its steel-wool prickle, that week-long unholy terror
of unpaid tithes or attention
               as recompense.

       As a child I sat in stealth,
hiding from God's glare in the church loft, upper left side,
where in a human body
             the recalcitrant heart
is found, and where in our near-lapsed Lutheran congregation
the stubborn organ pumped out heavy-handed hymns,
       the doubting young pressed into song
like smote choirs of angels, relieved
             to hear our own strained voices
mouthing the word *rejoice*
after the silent, spare moments
       of prayer for those passed away, the litany
of small, nervous coughs, whisper
of clean clothes chafing—
             but I was afraid,
     felt snared, caught between
a hot forever foxtrot with the hairy Devil
or the dangerous gift—like proffered candy
     from a scarcely-robed stranger—
of an endless roaming among sheep and clouds,
         the scatter of our small, winded souls.
It was clearly a trick, the offer
        of *being saved*—
the dark and unknown
     posing as white dove sprung from a black hat
and then not moving, never taking flight,
          stunned by the release.
       I wanted to run outside, leach my restless spirit

beyond the tall windows, red-stained
                         with Christ's suffer-all,
         wanted to escape the pulpit's double-talk
of consequence, even beyond this diminished life,
                              especially beyond—

         When would it ever stop? This taunting
of death, like some school yard lout on every chased street—
the second-grade boy with whooping cough
         already taken, his heart stopped from the on-and-on retch,
and then vaunted heaven, with its hoops to jump through
              came for my flawed parents
                         in a cold snap—with gunshots, a good deal of snow
and fair warning—
                   turned them to stone.

         Last Sunday my dog died
from the shock of her dark, clotted spleen
floating in rags around her bloodied intestines,
                   and a long-held friend, who's won
marathons—both the foot race and figurative sort—
boasts a brand new, out-of-body colostomy
and continual sensation of jet lag
                         as though she's flying against the sun,
swears that her next tilt at eternal life
                         will not be incontinent.
         Her brief school-girl joy
at having finished at least one thing, Hardy's novel
         of the *madding crowd*, memorable in the old movie spin off
for Julie Christie's beautiful, trembling mouth
              and its doubtful moral, love and solace
coming to a woman in middle age (on the palliative ward)
         like sheep muddling on a hill, seemingly by chance,
not choosing—
              no suitor finally her bellwether;
although her estranged husband lay with her ancient body

as late as yesterday—they shone like nested spoons
                        in a dark room opened to the light.

                She's circumspect, and why not,
feels the doctors threw her out of hospital
                to die at home among wracked family
as a last-ditch penalty
for removing the sign on her door, "No more than two visitors!"
                "Now they'll be sorry," she chides,
like a fizz-haired child at the centre of some sick-bed universe
who can't easily be replaced,
                                "no more reckless drinking
of ginger ale or night-long card games, winner takes all!"
                And maybe it's the mounting pain, or morphine—
                but neither of one of us/can remember,
whether Sundays are at week's end
                or time's beginning,
when the word was apparently God, and everything was
topsy-turvy, turned to salt or blossomed
                light, all those rumours of Adam and Eve
lollygagging around paradise in a windfall of apples,
the world broken open—
                                and then that sound,
a shrieking wind, warm gusting
of anger, as when a parent's love isn't enough—
                                we can't remember, either one of us,
now that her liver's shot, her feet swelling,
whether fear came at the right time
                                or still later.

Dedicated to the late Marilyn McClinton, 1940–2004.

NUCLEAR FAMILY

Train Wrecks, Rare Fossils

When I first saw them, slipped
from his woollen swim trunks, so shamelessly
war-time and loose at the inner thigh,
                              I was surprised
to find what finally made a man
                    a man, this bruised fruit
like something forgotten in a lunch pail—
                    this was what all the fuss was about
when the boys clutched themselves, keeled over
in mock pain like big cry-babies.

That every boy who taunted me
                    should have an awkward, jiggering set
of something akin to my mother's
bitter tulip bulbs (I'd once tasted one on a whim)
          well, it seemed a cruel joke
how I'd flowered into being
                    as a wary child.

And when in September
the teacher asked us, restless one by one,
          to name the things learned in our summers away,
a few swept faces clearly coy or lying
          in reports of train wrecks or rare fossils,
                    I thought of my father,
that puzzlement of flesh and flounce between his legs,
his frailty bared,
                    and wondered how my mother did it,
kept him safe;

when once I'd believed my father
          secret and entire—
                    someone to be watched
in a fearless diving from the bright shore
into the dark, stirred waters—
                              and said nothing.

Nuclear Family

"a popular term after World War II, describing the enclave of a father, mother and children, but of course the mushrooming bomb came to mind, as if those who loved hardest at the family's heated core might spin off from one another…"

—Anonymous

we were divided, I knew that,
tattling girls huddled in knots against
the recalcitrant boys until push came to shove
            and we fell hard for someone, switched sides—
the dandlers nuzzling by the goal posts
        made brave by the prospects
of drinking their parents' gin and going all the way
        and never mind their slim chances
at real joy being seeded
in morbid marriages, crying mothers
               black-eyed in the kitchen
and fathers, always misunderstood,
              vying to leave and who cared

we had to choose our battles—that much was clear;
       a girl getting the strap
with her insolent, slipped-down knee socks, near-flat chest
as rarefied a thought as a man on the moon—
           I thought it would change everything

        moonwalk, my version:
              I was duped
into helping a boy who couldn't spell (he had sweet eyelashes)
blaspheme a teacher royally
        in blue chalk beneath the Queen's portrait,
the affronted principal, a mad light in his eyes,
grunting with each lashing of my open hands, *do you want more? do you want more?*
           daring me

to flinch, turn away the world—
                    even then, when I knew nothing
of a tenderness found somewhere in the mix
            of love's blows,
                        it seemed like first, glaring sex

hot palms held before me like quaking trophies
I was returned to class, barely redeemable
                        in late October of 1962
and mistook the haunted look on the boys' faces, awed
to have a mere gash of a girl take the rap;
                    they were on their knees, hiding
behind their desks, in case US bombs were dropped over Cuba
or Russia smoked us all, nuclear-style—
                        and I was to do the same—
Duck down!
                shouted that teacher of late *cocksucker* fame
as I dropped to the floor near the boy I adored,
heels pressed against the white cotton dithering in my crotch,
                    my fingers still flaming

the world to be covered, we were warned,
with a hot driven snow, blizzard of ash,
                        all of us sheltered underground, and existing
on small packets of Kellogg's and powdered milk;
we would persist in the chastened dark
                    like endless nights of home movies
when something always went wrong,
            my father fuming at the flickering film,
his family projected as unremarkable archive—

        we were to be
                    locked in with our memories,
to avoid mutations, leathery scales and webbing, flightless wings,
        like the first addled creatures to crawl aboard
continents of swamp and stone—
                        we were to *live*, that was the point—

growing old and grating on each other's nerves
       as we had in our stark wartime bungalow
with the roughed-in rec room, a stale piano and outgrown puppet theatre
as proof of our brief childhoods
          ending in curfew, harsh critique
behind the shaded windows (my father's worst fear
        that we might be found lacking, only shirkers in Canada);
it seemed a worse fate than endless winter,
hiding like that (from ourselves, or so it seemed,
           as though the enemy were within)

      everything the same after thrilling nuclear war
except without a backyard of wild trees (all the squirrels
        and birds would go missing),
and all the older boys prone to stealing cars and setting fires
      still gloating in their tough skins
among the rumoured warrens and bunkers, skirmishing
for stolen food, speechless
           and unabashed as marauding reptiles
from a forgotten ice age (the girls still
intended to become make-do nurses or teachers
      until they married one of the dinosaur-boys
who finally came up for air)

           so I reared up
from my cubbyhole against incoming missiles,
      waving my arms
as though I finally had the right answer
to a fielded question about broken space
          and darkened time—

    I didn't know what war was, only family

My Father's Hat

some stand up to it, some don't
my father says, driving savagely, zigzagging through the choked lanes
the lakefront expressway in Toronto under construction
since I was a clueless kid
it looks like a war zone, that broken up
so my father's on a rampage, he doesn't like reminders
he's almost daring a cop to pull him over
have a little chat about authority—
a speeding ticket, a call to clobber people in the streets,
to him it's all the same thing, a menacing show of power
and it makes him spitting mad
how some people cave, in cowardice
or cheat their way to the top of the heap
sway in their beliefs about goodness or grace
cater to those with clout, sporting some gimcrack uniform
and you have to stay sharp, keep your head,
he reminds me, when someone asks for your papers, make sure
you're not on the losing side of things

I know, I say, lambasted into my seat
by the G-forces of his reconnaissance through the raw city
I know, because my grandmother (on my mother's side)
was small-time famous for refusing to say *Heil Hitler!*
never raising her deft arm in desperate salute
three times she landed in prison
worried to death about leaving the children
but she couldn't live with herself otherwise—
probably the shortest person in the clink with an attitude
even some of the steel-eyed henchmen admired her spunk
'cause that runt, Hitler, was still out there
rampaging on his tank in one of his fanatic parades
all that spittle when he was shouting
his zealot's claptrap about the human race

I wanted to raise bees, it would have been easier
my father says, when we finally hit
a side street, quiet, with overhead trees, and park
even that, with a fury, he's edging into a tight spot
cursing all the drivers in Canada, who take so much for granted—
our family came from farmers and school teachers,
he reminds me, peaceful people, who kept to themselves
he's almost forgetting we've arrived
at a small shop to restore his fedora, a pinched grey felt
and sometimes, under its shadow, he smiles a little

a man without a hat is no one, he's always insisted
meaning he's conflicted, might have been
somewhat proud, at seventeen, to be a paratrooper
with that telltale Kraut cap on his head,
dark serge with a patent-leather visor, spread-eagled insignia—
he had a hard landing, cracking three ribs in Crete
and later, shrapnel in his knee, lodged in his skull
all that spare time on his hands for reading
(or so he claims, Kant's theory of duty versus the horror of action)
while he was hiding, holding out
for something important to happen
it's the waiting that kills you, he's always said

I'm not yet seventeen, but I know
my father drives fast, headlong, that he's an angry man
and could hurt someone, and what he means
is that when you're young, and waiting
for someone else to make up your mind,
it hurts to breathe

Women in December

"It was reported their singing resembled
the flight of moths in moonlight.
Who can say? It is silent now."
                    —"What Were They Like?" Denise Levertov

Late in the uncompromising year
someone who sounds an awful lot like my sister—
there's that twang of the misbegotten, and she seldom
uses her real name—phones long-distance, collect:
                    she's at the bar
with a tender-hearted soft-porn producer named Mickey
                    (they both wish they were in Cancun)
and on a rant about a heavy fog in her locale, so thick
                    she can't make out who's who,
but maybe she'll weather it, the sensation
                    of feeling remote to the here and now;
        I counter with a slick riming of frost
where I am, glib on my mountainside
                        in expectation of snow,
soon I'll be getting out the shovel, I tell her,
implying how Christmas should be wrought—
        it's clean slate time
                    and you have to work for it. Dig deep.

        Last time I checked into our cliff-hanger
family—someone always diving, headlong,
        to avoid ambush at the edge—
                it was best to forego all celebration,
pretend nothing more perfect or beautiful
was at stake than coming home late
        or not at all; by caring less you had a chance.
But old habits die hard,
        like my mother did at my father's feet,
festooned in red, the strafing of snow that night
        into windswept drifts barely enough
                            to whiten things up.

Immaculate, my ass,
says my errant blood relative, her acid laugh
      reminding me that Mary was a woman of ill repute
before Joseph, the old codger, snapped her up,
as though she knew her personally while living on the street.
        It sounds all too familiar:
in her version, the wise men were drug dealers of feel-good frankincense
      who never showed, the night was without stars,
the baby died, trampled among the restive animals,
        and it's all about the taxes.
She's liquored up, querulous, thinks these thoughts original.

      It always surprises me
that despite our lack of sweetly expressed
        love (it's more likely fumed or vented)
we might sound like quasi-normal ilk and kin,
      overly anxious at year's end, recanting
how long it's been and who could better afford
the airfare, or forbearance,
        parsing words like *marzipan*
and *manipulate* in the righteous tone
reminiscent of misspent family, as though we could still
      right the wrong, everybody gets what they deserve,
her blame soon fraying toward hectic
      over my long and longer prologues
of silence—
      Are you listening? There's a microphone
in my drink—I can hear people talking about me,
      but it's all just rumours, she warns,
mistaking white noise for betrayal,
      insight with brief fame.
I run with her notion of a bad connection—
        and hang up.

It's like winter lightning between us,
      and maybe it began when we were young
and desperate, on a night of thunder-snow—
      but it's true that remembered pain

does strike twice, scares me away
from requisite praise, any small concession
to the woman who swears each year
she'll give me a raucous tattoo, pierced somethings,
          some new wound or scar
to bind us, sister-remnants of a lost clan;
                    so I know enough
to ring up a few friends in Toronto, keep the line busy,
      hear the fresh scraping of skate blades on ice—
they're on a pond in a real cold snap, no end in sight,
and glad for this spurring of abandon,
                 the almost-childish sensation of the surreal—
and never mind who's already fallen and bashed a chin,
          they're in the thick of it, in high spirits.

And I know that my daughter
suggests going to the abbey's midnight mass
          for the wicked music, as she calls it,
she's ready for some old-fashioned Christmas amaze—
and we're not Catholic, not anything
                 but deal makers with zazen,
still can't help ourselves sometimes in dark December
      from getting dolled up in head coverings and good coats
                       for the baby Jesus;
then stay home after all
          to watch a replay of the Three Tenors
coming back for encores in a balmy weather strangely like summer,
evening-gowned throngs by the Eiffel Tower,
          the catamount songs weary in translation
from old sorrows to tainted television.

      And when it grows late
              I know we linger,
waiting for the promised snow beyond the black windows,
      doing our best to beat the odds
amid the season's spoils, the festive slatherings of turkey
in all the wintered houses merely

                         a famished feast;
no one can get enough
            of the stilt mystery wrapped in doubt,
like an itchy sweater that doesn't quite fit,
                    might be better on a stranger.

This I know best:
                 how we will remember
as mother and daughter, pressed close,
        the fire on the hearth fallen to ashes,
our reading aloud, in stricken voices
the Levertov poem posing steep questions
                    of our living among the dead,
what we might say to them, in turn,
those spirits flown from our lost wars
                    to other realms of order, and light
in their soaring detachment
                    from the ornaments of joy,
        blackened lanterns of stone.

            For Alexis, who gave me the Levertov book one Christmas.

Tennessee Waltz

                    Call me romantic, a woman
who would wear a slant feather in her hat—
                              and *nothing but* a hat—
if the weather shone, she waving goodbye
        from an open casement or widow's walk
to some fellow cutting a figure, standing alone
among a crew of rascal sailors agape
                    at her slender waist and blown kisses.
        Call me ridiculous, stuck
in another time and place with finicky tastes
                        in the spoils of perfection, but I still believe
in staying true, just ask any one
            of my scores of bed-shakers and leave-takers,
persuasive *fellows of the law,* double-dealing
                in matters of contingency, or *faculty fellows,*
so cock-a-doodle-doo in retreat, quoting Baudelaire
in a petulant last doorway speech, wondering
                        who, in the end, gets the stereo. My stereo.

                    Rebuffed and rebounded,
I've abandoned a few hangers-on, neatly called it off
when they were found too morosely
                            married, real sticks-in-the-mud—
            or still boyish, at forty, with their odd habits of leaving,
as hostage or shameless reminder, their knocked-about hockey pads,
boxes of black-and-white photos (old girlfriends gone mouldy),
                    or when they proved themselves
too adamant (with tendencies toward stalking)
or absent-minded, standing me up
        with grand excuses: mail fraud, motels without clocks
or, get this, his professor in Comparative Lit lending him
        a proper cadence (and venereal warts).
I grew impatient,
                    like young Dracula with his striking cheekbones

last Halloween, his work visa almost expired.
I need a *vicarious viife,* he said, with a nice drool of blood
at the corner of his smile. I think he meant *virtual,*
or maybe *virtuous,* as in, a good reason to stay in the country.
       Never mind, we danced all night.

  My ill-suited suitors brainy
as all get-out, poets met on Sundays in bookstores,
wringing bright new sounds from the commonplace,
then falling back on old clichés
   of bones and bees, being stung first.
Speaking in soliloquies, like Ling Po or Catullus;
not quite what I had in mind
   when I urged for *a thousand nights with a Latin lover*
in a series of clever haikus. But forget the low times,
drinking Benylin in a proscribed red slip
and ripping the collars off his Oxford-cloth shirts,
   he gone with "the wife" (be careful of pronouns)
to hear that old crooner, Tony Bennett. I preferred
comical professors with flip-flop Irish accents, trotting about naked,
   hitting their own backsides, *giddy-up,*
to make fun of those "bloody Americans," even though
they, as well, wanted to inhabit an outlaw fame.
        Dreamed of making it big.

Lapsed Mormons, Catholics, pacifist Quakers,
     they were nonetheless spiritual, oh my God, yes,
fell for the whole Madonna-whore shtick,
a woman in a library thoughtfully loosening her long hair
having them go off half-cocked in reverie
     of sudden self-improvement,
seeing their reflections in pipe-smoking, Shetland wool sweater
literary fame, or starting up grunge bands of hard blues
bound to get out of North Bay one day and hit the El Mocambo,
the no-name rockers always breaking up over the girl singers
(I know that for a fact), or thinking themselves remarkable, *real artistes,*
splishy-splashy in their use of crashing colour and binge drinking,

like copy-cat Jackson Pollocks
                    with quicker tempers, smaller brushes.

They had little staying power, I'll say that much,
          this jaded crew, blaming their fathers
for undeserved private school with high expectations,
          or poor salesmanship in the jukebox trade
(they'd wanted to grow up in Palo Alto);
doctor's-bag-toting drug addicts claiming to be clean,
          bush pilots decrying the need for maps or direction,
so they could land, in all innocence,
          in some northern woman's backyard,
or trawlers of near-fishless rivers, holding out, as truce,
the slim silver lining of the bloodied catch;
                         they were all bound to fail—
unlike the scoundrels in their touted film noir—
                         in being found redeemable;
my fellows likely dog lovers,
skirmishing in their Nam war-resister fatigues
          with the fake-ferocious Alsatian
and hobbyist detractors from everything, even *bad news,*
making prickly moments of "Fuck you, too!"
          seem like a friendly walk in the park—
                    my attentive boyfriend of the moment
suddenly the bad guy, the mugger,
running off with my greatest treasures, my spilled beans
          and my teeny-tiny family,
                         all those wasted eggs.

I was crazed by them, one by one,
          the endless charm in calling their bluffs,
letting them off the hook as *sweet fellas*
          in loosened bolo and kicked-off boots
if they turned out to be broke cowboys, only drifters,
or gay.
                    And right now, I'm not having sex

with a man I've never met in Michigan—we correspond
like some on-and-on Tennessee waltzing of words
              on the world wide web, a surprisingly
                     springy surface, like those oh-so-forgiving
horsehair floors in old-time dance halls, the twirling couples
lifted in the moment, never tiring
                                    of the elegant hustle to stay in time.
        Call us whimsical—
                     a scot-free twosome without memory
of awkward bowling-lanes date, all that bending
              and later lunging embrace;
        no stunning red dress or teary dispute
                     over stung pride and who pays, a deal breaker
the one, and not the other, always fiercely denies.
        We share only the strange attraction
of taking note, it's all written down,
                     the things already missed:
we've never, for instance, leaned in
              and slurped a common strand of spaghetti
or caught the other asleep, as self-unaware
                     as a drooling and still-perfect child,
and once, in autumn, on a profoundly dark continent,
              we both stared up at the moon's blooded eclipse,
wrote to each other, three hours and two thousand miles apart,
using terms like *penumbral* and *"Did you see that?"*
        knowing the Saros cycle, a time span
of eighteen years, eleven days and eight hours
found to elapse before the planets nicely line up
              to be a long shot between us.
Still, we defy the usual flighty couple's tendency
        toward impermanence; sometimes we use real paper
just to nail things down on a thin matter of fallen trees,
        scribe of the unfinished business of children—
his and mine—
              our slim chances of ever knowing anything,
then sign our names, lick stamps.

By unlucky coincidence and unflattering
                            consequence, I have learned
that a *fellow* (according to etymology's garb)
                            is either *a man or a boy,*
at times a *beau* or *suitor,* an advocate
for old-fashioned rhetoric, really laying it on, addressing
        all the salient points like a love essay on legs,
or quite simply, *a person.*
                    Someone you see on the street, a complete stranger
until he leaves his mark, has gallantly given
some weary young mother his seat on the bus,
        the way he stands, swaying, smiling to himself—
you make a mental note
                        to revisit him in some fantastical future, have him
nicely knotted in your bedclothes, grant him
a small gesture of right response;
                            for some reason he gives you hope.

        That same man might be
a person of small worth or no esteem,
        as the lexicon also states, you just never know.
Dictionaries behave as if you *do know,*
        as if life's a case of what *is*: a table being a table, a horse a horse,
despite both having broad backs, an air of required patience.
Yet there are always new shades of meaning,
        language—and even the male species—constantly evolving,
a woman perhaps lying *on* a table (pedestal, red mahogany, circa 1920s),
                    her panties shucked, and a man
moving like a horseless rider
                            impatient to get home,
his fingers wet in her salt-and-sweet-chutney smell—
then a table might suddenly whinny, or buck a man off,
canter away into the next room
                            seemingly full of joy.
And the upstart in pursuit might be
                laughing, with something yet to offer

or might be another sort entirely, silent and undaunted,
a person belonging to the same rank or class,
her *equal,* her *peer*—
                    an outdated notion, perhaps, with everyone these days
showing so little regard,
but I fall for Clive Owen in every one of his films,
                    cast as croupier, or servant, reaching beyond
his so-called station in life, his best shot
at impressing a woman always
                                        his pure, dark emotion.

        I like the thought, too,
of a *fellow* being a *companion, comrade,*
                    like a harmless father, beloved brother,
boy next door and painfully faithful dog all rolled into one.
Last, but certainly not least,
        a *fellow* might be considered a fellow of *mine,*
as *one of a pair, mate, match:*
                            someone who arrives, and belongs,
chastens a woman
like a warming hand inside a glove
                    for not having been found sooner,
the season without   so achingly cold.

Would You Rather

I.

We're hung up in traffic over the Second Narrows,
      glint water below, ambivalent sky
shifting its premise in bright cloud above,
      so we're killing time, my daughter
setting me trappy riddles of either-or, her version
                of Zen-as-suffering. "It's like choosing
deaf or blind,"
          she says, as prologue to her rough game,
and we both laugh, although
there's something at stake
        in putting her mother on the spot.
She's almost seventeen, and restless, I get that.

        She gives me Africa: would I rather
dig wells, quench a whole continent's thirst—
it's back-breaking work, bound to end
      in despair, or at best
a caring-for-others award, there might be comfort in that—
        or would I rather
                have wings?

"There's no flying," she's quick to add,
"you're too heavy and geeky, an emu-person,
almost extinct—
      you just *have* wings.
Prickly, scrunched up beneath sweaters,
a real stickler for your wardrobe."

I want to say, life's not like that,
but it is—one option sounding vaguely noble
        and flight seeming elegant, the easy way out—

I'd take blind," she says, urging me
                    to take the leap.
          Swears otherwise she'd miss her music,
that boy with a keening high voice
          who lately walked, fully dressed, into the Mississippi,
sings more like an angel now than ever.
          And the *Emperor Concerto*, Beethoven
having lost all hearing and composing the piece under siege
          by Napoleon—so he knew the odds.
I feel like she's choosing sadness and memory
                    over heroics. Why is that?

Her hearing's fine, eyesight ideal.
She had a rating of ten out of ten for kicking and screaming
                    when she was born,
the chaplain stopping by to see what shape I was in
          as a single mother, spiritually.
                         Grateful, I think I was,
and hungry to boot, hollowed
          by relief at her thrilling escape,
the good doc having told me my child was likely
          hydrocephalic (water on the brain)
and there was scant hope either way, by taking her early
or leaving things too late.
               I followed my hunches,
hung on full term to deliver a perfectly-formed
               prankster, daring me
not to shorten the game, wring its proud neck.

     Wings it is then, over water.
I smile like one of the already afflicted,
                    dreaming my feathers beautiful.

II.

But that's not the end of it.
We're driving long miles back from Vancouver,
admiring our new getups, her waist-length hair chopped
      and mine bruised with colour, to hold back
my life story, its latest nuance of gun-metal grey:
                        she's reading to me, aloud,
above the chuffed air from the open windows,
      an old sixties' novel, *The Favourite Game,*
melancholic Cohen, in all his youthful angst of what to do
      and soon (it always comes to this)
            we're in the thick of it, the inscrutable
questions, her raised eyebrows, each time—
                      "Wings? Really?"
as if surprised by this new mother, when pressed.

                 "Would you rather,"
she begins, "give up reading—
          no more Vanderhaeghe or Henry James,
or poetry either, no Raymond Carver or good old Yeats,
no Saturday *Globe* or browsing of cereal boxes;
              you'll be housebound, a shut-in,
there's no driving without road signs, unless you win the lottery,
      get yourself a small, balding chauffeur—"

      I laugh off the notion.
Why couldn't a windfall grant me a younger, taller man
           for wicked road trips?
I step up the fantasy, see myself in motorcycle leathers
            pressing against the wind, and I'm the bad-ass driver
on the lam from reading, knowing each bright new thing
            in the passing landscape, as if by heart.
"Or what—?
      What's my other daunting option?"

She hesitates for effect,
wants in the long run, to study history—or theatre—
can't decide.
                    "Or would you rather
            give up writing?
                No deadlines with frazzled editors,
no small fame in literary mags, not even
            private scribbles. Forget your dreams
of the Giller, the thank-you speech or new oooh-lah-lah dress;
            you don't have to struggle anymore—"

I bristle at her goddess-stuck-in-high-school
            voice, the one that says,
Look sharp, I'm calling the shots.
                She's neatly upped the ante, and this time
there's no squirming out, no fudging the answer.
The pretending of free will
                    feels real. Nothing but
            a hard place, crushing choice.

I picture myself as mother-turned-monk,
                living in privation in Tibet, bells ringing
as calls to my acquiescence.
                        Then breaking loose
from the silence, the terrible insight required
            and writing down the first thing that comes into my head.
And suddenly I say,
                "Smell the grass,"
a heady fragrance of fresh-mown hay coming off the fields,
and she breathes, and breathes
                        and I do too.

WHEN THE POWER WENT OUT

Which One of Us, in White

We have not yet begun—
this brazen heaping of spring snow
        so bitterly cold
even the chastened warblers
and Steller's jays, small finches at the feeder
            have nothing to say.
Cards, for example, we have not yet
played Kings in the Corner or Crazy Eights.
        We have not given occasion
to a stirring of hot chocolate
the old-fashioned way, with clumped cocoa,
milk simmering in a saucepan.
                Or spoken of our mothers, for that matter.
The old board games—Scrabble, Monopoly?
Who *is* tending Park Place these days,
raking in the loot from the Burlington & Ohio Railroad,
dabbling with uneasy luck in high-spirited
scrimmage at the boundaries
        of what we have long named "the real world"?
        Who is inventing unscrupulous
words just to see the look of astonishment
        on another's face? *Carab*?
(Yes, that beetle the Egyptians laid over the hearts of corpses.)
                You don't believe me?
Scarab then.
        (Or *sarcophagus*.)

We have faltered, in our wonder
                at the quiet, white kernel
folded inside the wider scene of buried lawn chairs
and marbled gardens, mounting drifts
        surrounding the house—a clean slate of silence.
We could scarcely now
        find enough scarves and mittens,
even imagine

lying down   and making angels
in the crystalline gardens, our foolish faces
          tilted toward the steeled air,
the snow sliding (in small shocks) up our spines
in our curious flapping

                    and flapping,
our fledgling shapes trying to rise.

          And what of ill-formed igloos,
looking like sorry half moons, or a lopsided snowman
          leaning toward the back stoop, as if
awaiting the haberdashery of carrot-nose, lumps of black coal
                    as wintered eyes? ·
     It's a shame to think
no toboggan will soon be tugged along
          for heave-ho descent from the high pastures,
our shouts of "Tree!" or "Hold on!"
               ringing against the dazzled white slopes.

And last night, when the power went out,
                    which one of us
watching stopped clocks, stunned
by the prospect of a creeping chill on all the floors,
the window panes frozen by morning,
          which one of us
not yet deserted by the will for this profound weather
               crept to the cold hearth,
a stash of sweet-tooth marshmallows in hand,
and started up a smart fire,
                    which one leapt outside
as if on a glorious hunch—haunted
          by some childish or ancient oracle—
     tore at the limbs of the aching trees,
brought in from the cold
               a tribe of sharp, pointed sticks?

Dedicated to the late Bud Allison, 1921–2018.

The Odds

The other day a Russian man—former spy
           so he could never go home—jumped
from the rooftop of a high-rise in Montreal, holding hands
with his wife of I don't know how long
                    and a boy,
       a bond of duty or perhaps
the married pair had been childhood sweethearts,
       crazy-passionate since forever,
the stepson, at fifteen, suddenly facing
                    none of the problems of youth,
his hemming and hawing toward recklessness
       already complete.

           Their story was small
on the newspaper's back page, with a grainy photo
of a grey building, dark gaping windows, no curtains,
the sharp line of the roof
       bleeding in with the puzzled sky.
I had to wonder at the configuration: was the boy
in the middle or off to one side, the two lovers
       joined at the hip? And who
was more afraid? Were all finally willing?
                    The odds are against
any threesome sharing the same drummed-up
       comedy of flight; it's hard enough
for two to hold fast any notion bound to endure
fifteen storeys in free fall, legs jerking
                    against the steepness of freedom.

       I wanted to speak with them briefly,
fuss over them, as if in a final photo—have one
           step back from the edge,
another manage a stiff smile, and longed to say,
"This won't work, you're all backlit by the sun.
                    We'll have to try another day."

I could see no way to spare the woman and child.
The man was clearly at the centre of it,
                no stragglers, no one left behind.

Were there shouts, whispers, songs *a cappella*?
Was there a signal to begin,
                a chanting of Russian verse as entrance to the air?
Brodsky perhaps? A reminder that *one can't
    step twice into the same cloud*?

I didn't quite believe the commotion, dreaded
being persuaded. Felt the need
                to roar with laughter
at the way we are grand—in our conceptions
of spirit over matter, of being saved—
                                    and then not.
The conniptions, the crumbling.
The agonizing rush to meet grief and loss,
                pure attention to gravity.
        Were their eyes open or closed?
It's possible that one was amazed at the halfway mark
                while another felt oddly amused
a sweet split second before hitting the ground
with an emphatic harvesting sound of ready human fruit.
The third terrified all the way down, wanting still
        to be whole and unbroken.

        The Russian, whatever his former miscreant life,
imagined the chin-wagging prime minister to be plotting
against him, poisoning him in his dingy water pipes—
the tenement where the newcomers were stashed
        looked a real shambles. Despite this
distracted theory, he seemed articulate, well dressed,
even elegant in demeanour while under threat of deportation.
        So say his few friends and his immigration lawyer.
Seems you can never tell when a crack a mile wide
                might open in someone.

I think the well-loved Russian—
and he might have been, to pull off such a stunt—
        missed a cue to his own played-out performance
as god-like, or sick-at-heart scapegoat,
                        the sacrifice of others
        a bitter antidote to doubt.
                Felt his ears drain in the spun dark
with that little popping and gurgle sound
        they make at high altitudes, when something releases,
all the things he'd been hearing as bleary echoes
become crystal clear. A metallic taste in his mouth,
the smoky flavour of his own blood.
                And the rest of us left with the shame.

Anyway, I took the story—this strained family's descent—
        as omen. Decided not to keep the baby.
Yes, the doctor said, I see.

Freshet

I.

A cold spring,
unflinching in its hold on leaf-furl and fledgling,
the highlands of the Chilcotin still stockpiling the white stuff
in late May, flurries wheeling down the Coquihalla
and here, in the glommed-on suburbs east of Vancouver—
this flood plain once the "Berry Capital of the World"—
there's a sense of waiting in the dark, the morning
commute inching its way toward the Pacific,
all the slippery melt-work
yet to come—
ice heaving in the Nechako up country, and of a sudden
it's summer in spate,
a roiling warm spell,
cars pulled up along the banks of the Fraser—
people want to see for themselves,
stand by the river's race, the waters rising—
record watermarks etched on the iron rule
by the old CP rail bridge, once the sole spanning of the muddy spree
a half-mile wide at the tide line in Mission,
and later become a single-lane car crossing—*toot, toot!*—
withstanding the great flood of '48
only to collapse on a whim, the piers buckling
in slow motion, seven years later;
so you never know.

There's that pitter-patter of fear,
like cat's paws on the surging water, people resorting
to common sense for a change,
moving backyard pleasure horses and llamas, goats, sheep
up the slopes, the local hardware sold out
of lanterns and batteries, buckets, back-up generators,
all the small talk on the street
of rip-rap and run-off—

the experts churning out lazy graphs
contemplating snowpack and real-time flowage,
the science of *bathymetry* from Big Bar to Tranmer
                    ringing poetic, the river's *confluence*
near Harrison Knob, or its *avulsion,* the main channel shifted
by Herrling Island, the *echo soundings*
as measure of the *heavily braided* gravel reach upriver, towards Hope,
or sweet mention
                    of *the falling limb* of the freshet,
when the peaked waters—and we're nowhere close—
start receding,
          the giant Fraser (its watershed the size of Great Britain)
                    as hard as the shifted weather
                                        to predict;

          just ask the river-witchers, those screwball
squatters under the bridge trestle, their eyes wild
with want—in their doleful regard
                              the ground *is* water,
they can *feel* the freshet (it's not rocket science),
          hear the urgency in the water's dissent
between the aching bridge-piers, they're under a spell
watching its teeming spackle,
                    a deluge almost a given,
they've wished this heat wave, are calling the water down
                    from the ice-spurred hills, a feeling of near-debacle
makes them feel right at home,
the night freights passing over their strafed sleep
                    like the shunting end of the world—
they've heard the rumours steeped at Tim's
where the gang gathers because the TV ads talk to them
like a fast-food family, everyone in a rush
and hepped-up high spirits,
                              almost *too high;*

like the mayor, who knows the main drag
with its fusty old Sears store and depression-era post office

could disappear in a flash,
                              he's half hoping
the once shake-mill-town, more bust than boom,
          is finally on the map,
                    all those edgy headlines, reluctant heroes—
there's nothing like disaster
          to garner trickle-down funding
(the whole pretty scatter of houses against the mountains
                    could be cut off)—
so he's hamming it up, photo-ops galore
                    in the seeping pastures, bulldozers moaning
in a pell-mell raising of the berms, the diking roads
long since become pleasant riverside trails for cyclists and heron watchers,
          illicit venues for summer carousing—

          and despite the sand-bagging of the church
down on the flats last Sunday swelling the meagre congregation
(the pastor seizing an opportunity for contrition),
          it's a water lottery
and we've got all the right numbers for *an act of the Almighty*
          that moves us all, the water's cravings
for reach and rupture mounting the banks,
                    the past summers of spark and fire,
shorn forests red-tinted with pine beetle, the silted Fraser
undredged for decades (boaters hearing the water
          rubbing like sandpaper against the gunwales);
everything at stake and we're at odds
                    on how to treat a river:
the First Nations salmon fishers (the *Sto:lo, people of the flowing water*),
duck conservationists, farmers of strawberries and milk herds,
quarry miners and tree-loggers, wary newcomers
in their gated super-houses plunked on scraped hillsides
          and drained lake-bottoms—

it's latent baptism time,
prepare to be dunked by way of stream and rill

run oceanward for eight hundred miles;
we're long overdue
                    to find vintage sturgeon
docked on the living room sofa, unblinking,
         giant-fish-as-yogis
teaching us by stubborn example
                    to breathe slowly
against a strong current, take stock—
cherish
         what we might lose.

II.

                    Or as River Bob so neatly puts it,
graffiti-wise (complete with happy face ☺)
         What comes down, goes down. All the way
to the beautiful effing sea. Nada.
         His last word on the subject either Sanskrit
for *great river,* or Hemingway Spanish
                    meaning, *all for naught, nothing.*

III.

                    We're enterprising on the west coast,
dot.com know-it-alls, yoga-mindfully on-edge green,
                    big fans of big air and bicycles, glam movie-shoot locales,
thinking our no-logo notions of saving the planet
by way of *chia* and *chai,* slam poem, pipeline protest and pride parade
                    the right way forward—we just want
to live organically, free-range forever
                    in suspended youth, have little patience
with the lessons of the hoary past, or feeling settled;
we want, and want, and want
to live near water—
                    it's a tricking of the light,
the way it shimmers like an endless wave on the horizon,
we feel a hint of recognition—call it spiritual, if you want—

that's why we buy the view,
trudge toward it in our high-end hiking boots,
tend to go out of bounds on world-class mountains
                                    just to lose ourselves,
and God, how we complain,
                like unjustly served children,
want even the weather to indulge us—
you can see it in our strayed eyes, during long commutes
over grid-locked bridges, how we suffer
to get that promised buzz
                                of playing hard in paradise—
Shoring up is not our thing.

                We've lost the knack
            of finding water's source, well-dowsing
with a fresh-cut branch of willow or hazel
(although avid winemaker, Robert Mondavi, still doodlebugs),
                                    and have no inkling
of the heights and depths, water's big picture
when it falls and flows,
                                        how wet it finally gets.
We scarcely remember the clouds
learned in school, the stacking sort, upper layers
striated and flattened in the shape of an anvil
                        or vast plume. *Cumulonimbus?*
        Hardly anyone recalls
the silver gelatin prints of the daunting flood
in 1894. Or the mid-century photos of two young boys
            clinging to a sinking house front
upriver from Vancouver, near Hatzic.
                                    Their drained faces.
        We were all set in those days,
eyes glued to our brand-spanking-new console TVs, to celebrate
            finding water on the moon.

IV.

What *will* we gather up?
Scripted pills for effervescent moods of grab-and-go? Laptops
awash with eBay's flotsam and jetsam? Right shape-sorter or sucking
toys for fussing babes? Pictures of black-clad grandmothers
brooding within pewter frames? (They've seen it all,
the packing up in a fever pitch, last stand
         of cavalier pride.)

Food, and how much? Neighbours not so gallant
these days, and canned goods passé, mainly for pensioners
    and the poor—hardscrabblers or stranded sailors.
   And what of the sundry, indulged pets—what loyalties there?
Please, for goodness' sake, pack up the exotics,
we want no panicking arachnids, cockatiels, pythons—
       no swimming tigers in the streets.
And never mind entire herds of truly mad
cows, thousands sprung, udder-full, from their vast factory farms
   and bawling for help on higher ground; at least
they'll get to see real grass for a change,
    kick up their flummoxed heels.

   And what of the weather, what to wear?
What's *de rigueur*? A backyard barbecue of poached fish, served
à la mode in frothy, urban rain gear, with a splash of pinot gris?
How 'bout flip-flops, wrap-around batik skirts for that *laissez-faire*,
stuck-in-Bali-in-the-wet-season look?

     Or you might just call it a day,
remembering you were born
in the east, during Hurricane Hazel, your parents
   ashamed in their rubber knee-highs, bailing out
the basement, swearing not to abandon the shingled war-time bungalow
to its chastened fate—
    and when the house became unmoored,
the waters from the Humber rising so fast,

they had to suck it up, their immigrant pride,
and live for a time at the pastor's home,
        your father still remarking years later
on the lewd looks the cleric gave your shivering mother
in her clinging wet dress,
            and that's not the worst of it—

you've seen a woman in Malawi
on the late-night news, holding a baby in raised arms
above a raging river, even the air weeping—
        or those poor sods clinging to rooftops
during Katrina, waving and waving at Sean Penn in a rowboat
as though it were a movie, and they might make it
to the final cut, soppy Hollywood ending;
            later there were fourteen thousand stray dogs
and as many full-blown addicts
                rounded up, nothing merciful about it—

            it's a nasty bit of business, a flood,
full of mud and surprises, unrecognizable things
that look like inner tubes, but have fur or feathers—
        uprooted is the big sensation,
you're likely to see ancient trees, root ball and all, go floating by
or your neighbour's rust bucket of a truck,
            and you're suddenly knee-deep in it, what seems to be
freezing-cold human waste—

        Water, of course;
even with so much sluicing down the pike we'll all need
        to drink. The glass-half-full clean, sparkling sort.
We are fountains of the stuff—
            our startled hearts, awash
in the bloody mess of the riven moment—depend on it.
                And blinking, opening our eyes.

V.

On the east coast they're better prepared,
harbour a wealth of rain barrels, still, and ship-lapped dories
holding irascible once-cod-fishers
in foul weather gear, at the ready,
spouting stories as they row through the swells
of cruel Irish luck or Acadian ousting;
they know *how* to leave home, start over—
can slake a thirst
should the front porch come untethered
from the house, the whole plotted farm gone under in the welter,
and despite it being a cliché—they don't care—
they're clogging, dancing on a sheet of flown-about plywood,
the reel spun faster and faster in defiance,
the sharp fiddles creaking—
there's a revelry in taking a river by the throat
and stemming high water, staving off what's imminent
with a bright singsong
of names

by the St. Francis River at the Glasier Lake outlet, the Fish River
near Fort Kent, Grande Rivière at Violette Bridge,
the Iroquois at Moulin-Morneault, Aroostook
near Tinker, the Tobique River at Riley Brook, Meduxnekeag
near Belleville, Big Presque Isle Stream at Tracey Mills,
the Becaguimec at Coldstream, Shogomoc
near the highway that runs clear across Canada,
the Saint John, muddied at Maugerville, but running peaceably still
at Fredericton;

they are measuring the creek-spill
at Sandwith's Farm, the Nackawic Stream near Temperance Vale,
the Nashwaak River at Durham Bridge, and Narrows Mountain Brook
near the mountain's base, by the north branch of the Oromocto
at Tracy, and Salmon River at Castaway—

Have you had enough
        of this thrilling rigmarole
                                or would you still hear more?
The shirred warnings of brook and bend, sudden weddings
        of one ribald streaming to another,
these incantations
        of brined-up river shivaree:

Newcastle Creek at Grand Lake, the Jemseg River
at Jemseg, the outpouring of French Lake at what the locals call
The Corner, and the Saint John once again by Upper Gagetown,
the Canaan River at East Canaan, the Kennebecasis
at Apohaqui, the Lepreau at Elmcroft, and we haven't even begun
to quantify the water of the St. Croix at Baring, or Dennis Stream
near St. Stephen, the Grand Falls Flowage, the Restigouche
below Kedgwick River, the Upsalquitch,
or Nouvelle Rivière au Pont—

                        If you haven't paid your toll
for the miraculous, have merely
        crossed the bridge, over and over, inattentive,
have shamelessly taken a dip in some headlong
                moment as a child at the plummeting dam,
you'd better listen up:
                        now the intricacies matter—
of riddled shore, bruised wetland or untended
        weir, each outcropping of bedrock or barrage of windfall
unspared in the ruckus—
                        in this testing of resolve
at all the chastened banks and restive landings,
what was once a slow meander become furious lap-and-chase,
        bright risking of water—

along the Restigouche above Rafting Ground Brook,
Eel River near Dundee, Rivière Caraquet at Burnsville,
the Big Tracadie at Murchy Bridge Crossing, the Miramichi
running southwest at Blackville, the swill of the Catamaran at Repap Road Bridge,

the Coal Branch River at Beersville, and the Petitcodiac
both above and below the causeway, Turtle Creek
at the townsite of Turtle Creek, the Black River by Garnet Settlement,
the Point Wolfe at Fundy National Park, Carruthers Brook
near St. Anthony, Dunk River at Wall Road, the Wilmot in Wilmot Valley,
Winter River near Suffolk—

    let's pause for a minute, we're almost
at spring's shout, every liquid voice
                once baroque stream-song
now raucous hallelujah, Handel's symphony with tempo racing,
                     the horns recklessly off-key—

the Shelburne River at Pollard's Falls Bridge,
Moose Pit Brook by Tupper Lake, the LaHave at West Northfield,
St. Mary's River at Stillwater, the Northeast Margaree
in Margaree Valley, the Cheticamp above Robert Brook—
           hear the gauges dance
at Indian Brook, Middle River at Maclennan's Cross, and again
at Rocklin, the River Denys at Big March, the Kaministiquia,
the water rising by the Bear River at St. Margaret's, the Great Village River
near Scrabble Hill, the Kelly where Mill Creek enters at Eight Mile Ford,
the Tusket at Wilson's Bridge, the Rossway at Lower Ohio,
the Mersey below George Lake—

                  to sing out these signal streamings
is prayerful strategy, safety net;
           water is connected, after all,
by parsed farmlands on one side of the country
to industrial waste-landings on the other, cold rusings of fog
    swelling the ghosted shores with returning rains
coal-blown all the way from China.

VI.

The names are blessing,
or once were, marking abundance
where water was *found*
(and thanks be to an earlier God for that),
where stock was grazed, land tilled,
water as recourse, recompense,
a rinsing clean—of clothes, or smote skins,
unsettled scores—
where fires were stunted, and travel resumed—
in short jaunts willfully upstream, or down—small towns begun
with a stockpiling of goods, unfamiliar faces soon enough
a kind of startled kin;

the names eulogy as well,
when fur-laden canoes foundered or a buggy failed to cross,
where winter ice scraped
and darkened, and a well-worn stranger fell through,
a whirlpool of speculation then
about why he came to the region at all, what devious desire
of sullen homestead or strayed sweetheart
drove him through the unsparing weather—
The nomenclature
of numbing portage or precipitous breach
recalled as measure of the wealth or welcome
still to come, the splish-splashing
of feckless children in laxer seasons,
lurking of lovers on dulcet lip
of a once-reticent coursing—
there was implicit danger and promise of plenty, enough for all,
but no going back.

Here, in the unrepentant west,
the heat-musted valley finally spurred with green
and still no one happy—
farmers bound to lose the berry crop and first harvest of hay,

the rest of us with vacations on hold, up on our toes—
we stare at the far shore of the risen Fraser,
        watching the resolute tugboats
prying baleful debris from the bridge columns,
cast-off logs from booms, swirling tractor tires, riverside garden chairs,
            River Bob's water-scourged mattress leaving for the sea,
his scrawled happy face bleeding
                        toward amaze;
we are together, no longer apart
            in this new high regard for high water
in the far-flung reaches, the wrung-out curtains
            by the windowsills of the century-old house,
                wondering *if* and *if* and *if*
the river does its spectacular work with record risings
            of platinum waters, we will thrill to the real meaning of days,
our neighbours once more
                    become intimate, fragile
rushing around like the rustic hens in the receding gardens;
            this is *our* time, this June
not ten years downstream, but *now*, this crazed freshet
with its surfing deadheads and underwater snags,
            this is our one, lively certainty—

    we have *done* this, affected the world
with our heli-skiing at the very top, our hectic clear-cutting and off-roading,
our plumes of exhaust *just to return a video*—
            there's a hubris in that,
a Chevy-by-the-levee reckless lather
to feel alive—
            we have warmed to the notion
of twelve-thousand-year-old ice in our chi-chi cocktails (that fad
starting at Vancouver's Expo, west coasters
            slurping on chunks of glacier just to be cool),
        and we have rarely stopped
to see a beautiful thing
                    in its entirety, *as it is*—

yet we can still save
        the most delicate, or durable,
the flat-eyed feral cat whelping kittens in the attic,
        or those folks grown old by the river's chant
and now refusing
        to leave their restive homes (they recall
exactly where they were, that June day, with the breaching of the dikes),
we can lend a hand to the children in their preening games,
those who can't move fast enough
            to imagine the upshot;

and please throw River Bob and his cronies a coin
        for sniffing the wind
and showing us how it's done, how you bloody-well
        kick ass, survive the pandemonium,
scrounging among the busted-up boats, praying for either sunshine or rain,
you can't remember the odds, the flown time
        when you hedged your bets as a youth
and still won when you lost,
          still became everything—

      the waters are rising, yes,
but we can lift the young and the old
above the redoubtable river—
        carry them across, by recounting the names:

        starting with the headwaters,
the coursing of the Gregor, Raush and Robson rivers, the Willow
and the Bowron, the run of the Swift River, the San Jose and Horsefly
in the Cariboo-Chilcotin, the Chelaslie, Blanchet and Stuart
spilling into the ice-jammed Nechako,
        and tip your hats to the Yalakom, Nahatlatch
and Stein rivers, the Bonaparte and Nicola, Mad River
and Thunder River, the Deadman,

                    they're worrying
by the north and south arms of the Thompson,
the Eagle River soaring, as expected, the Shuswap, Seton
            and Hurley all going gangbusters, and don't be fooled
by the names of the Tranquille, or the Barrière,

and there's trouble
below Bridge River and the Coquihalla, in the narrow gulch
of the Fraser Canyon (never a body found alive
                        when taking a dunking at Hell's Gate),
and if, after Hope,
the waters widen, seem to slacken in the broad flood plain,
            there's still a mood of surprise
in the side channels, in navigating the fraught currents
around the sandbars and islands,
            you can see the every-which-way of flow
                        when looking east from Carey Point—
so take heart,
                there are forty-four gauges yet to come,
at McGillivray Slough, Chilliwack Creek at Wolfe Road,
Minto Landing by the Bell Slough, by Harrison Mills,
at Scowlitz and Hammersley, Wahleach Creek by the Powerhouse,
            and new measures of flowage at Tenas Narrows
on the Lillooet, at Lower Kent, north of Hunter Creek,
            and Minto Channel's always a tricky one,
or the back-spill by the Camp Hope Intake, the Agassiz-Rosedale Bridge,
folks still out for Sunday strolls on the dikes
            bound to be overtopped, this year or the next,
by the mudslinging Chilliwack,
                or that fisherman's reach, the Vedder Slough;

        the reckless creeks just as handsome
in effect, McConnell Creek fast flowing east of Mission,
or Cascade Falls just a hop, skip and jump up the road,
            the trick is staying grounded by the edge,
and don't let the family dog get swept away in the excitement,
wanting to be part of the fun during the freshet;

      it can happen while you're stunned
by the words you're dreaming up,

                    elegant sharp sounds
for *escape,* or *goodbye,*
you're searching for a likely name,
      water as *pooled light*—is there such a word?
water as *flag,* or *flume,*
       wet-whistled words for *scourge,* or *trickle,*
for *drenching,* or *thirst;*

         you are shouting syllables for water
in foreign languages, as if you've known them all along—
Uji! in Albanian, *Voda!* in Croatian or Czech, *Vand!* in Danish, or *Ama!*
 in Cherokee, *Shui!* in Mandarin, W*ai!* in Maori,
                   and *Jal!* in the Punjab;

        you are making plans
for playing besotted scrabble with the neighbours
               if you live through this,
bonus points for words like *rindle* or *runnel*—
you're thinking of ruin
         and of grace—

     the lovely *plink-planking* sound,
where we have stopped, by flashing water
in our plunders for gold or small fame, matters of family remittance,
     in our wanders for life's hardpan meaning,
in our seeking—it always comes to this—
         of shelter, our clinging to this earth
and giving thanks
        above the floating roar

Yesterday, I looked inside

a gold, late-model Grand Marquis, remember those?
The driver's keys, unclutched, on the seat
beside him, a little of his youth
still hesitant on his face,
                              his skin so blue—
the late afternoon fading as well in the early summer's
heat, the car's hazard lights
        blinking on-and-off, on-
and-off, relaying a last-minute
presence of mind—
                        and then doubt—
courage, and then a failing.

                Hard to know
whether he was coming or going—in a real flap
                        or taking his own sweet time—
the back seat crammed with a vintage red
vacuum, broken lamp and barrage of cardboard boxes
holding God-knows-what,
                the sum total of a kind of living.
A passerby laughed with me about that.
We took turns leaning into the car's open windows
                and shouting into the man's face.
That can sometimes be a lifesaver,
                even wrong-sounding words
better than a roaring white street
                                of silence.

                For some reason I thought
to recite a few poems
                        that might awaken a man:
one by Carver about the last years
                                being "pure gravy,"
and a few words from John Donne

on the subject of death being not especially "proud"
            while my cohort, curious as I was,
to see some trick of transparency—a lifting *up*
or *out of*, as easy to believe
                        as smoke from a winter chimney—
kept repeating, "Can you hear me? Are you
diabetic?" and once, just for a joke,
        "Hey buddy, here come the police!"

But there were no sirens,
        although we'd called for response;
the air hung heavily in the street, and the man
        didn't even twitch, not once,
while we yodelled and felt ill at ease,
                        a third bystander soon
sprinting to the nearby Big-B Saloon
(where the girls would start dancing later)
                to spread the news, some sorry sod
blacked out—maybe not even breathing—

        A quarter-hour tripped by
like soft, sullen eternity,
        an ambulance finally gliding into view—
it seemed cruel providence
to remember the milk I'd bought, spoiled in the heat.
        "You did the right thing,"
the paramedic said, pulling on his baby-blue latex gloves,
although I'd been afraid
        to touch a man with writhing-snake tattoos,
his mouth gaping—
        had offered only badly canted verse
                as resuscitation.
"He's a known drug user, has OD'd before,"
                the medic said, without blame,
as if despair were an accepted fact
like the earth being round
        and wobbling slightly on its axis.

We were standing in front of the Bellevue,
            a roughneck hotel survived
from boom-and-bust days in a lumber town,
cars slowing, faces craned
                  to catch sight of someone
unrecognized, and in real trouble—
                        that's as good as it gets, a thrilling
of blood, their own lives
            remarkably unscathed.
Maybe they thought I knew
the collapsed man, had chosen
            to love him, the way we do—helplessly,
and half-hearted—
                  or cheapened the story
once they got home, some drifter's
girlfriend or sister, bawling her eyes out
      on the main drag, they saw the whole thing.
I hate that, people blowing things
                  out of proportion. It shows us up
to be only passing strangers, nothing more.

            Believe me, it was this simple.
I saw the gold car, the blued skin
            of the man inside
                  and how he wanted
to prepare for beauty—
                  give it his best shot,
get somewhere without any hitches, for once,
without that shimmering hook, or hoop
that always snared him—
                  and such a quiet approach,
                              on old, bald tires.

Paradise, Later Years

Et alors?

Yes, and wasn't our dalliance
                    a real *promenade à cheval*?
Which might sound like a hokey small-town
parade, more ominous send-off to war, trumpets and drums,
horses clip-clopping over the underlying theme
of conquest, sacrifice.
                    But ours was a more
ticklish sallying-forth, think of the word
chevaucher.
                    In mundane translations
you'll find *straddle, ride,* etc. A horse, or chair.
There's no equivalent—in English—
                    of the French-speaking ability to *chevauche*:
(a horse, for instance, in allowing you
to sit astride...)
                    while finding oneself, *en se trouvant,*
nicely distracted by the motion, the passage itself,
or more acutely aware,
                    a horse skittish by nature, apt
to prance in fear as much as high spirits.
                    What's crucial in the notion
has to do with flow (not control),
with connection (not hierarchy). Think of a rider coaxing
the horse with treats and gentle aids, not spurring
it punishingly...
                    Another slant meaning
is *to overlap*. Finding ourselves
chevauchant: how nicely we cover each other,
                    and recover, re-cover.
                    Response at all the unknown edges of knowing.
This smudging of boundaries, no telling
          where we leave off
start to finish, end to end, top to bottom
in intimate tallyho, no one knows
                    who's leading the dance—
that's the closest we get:
                    how you sat on my lap

80

in the listing old Peugeot
(that was an elegant switch, he on she
in a non-churchlike position).
                    In fact you were light as a feather
and still strong, in holding back,
the way I learned
                            to think men were intended,
and it wasn't even raining along the coast,
                    felt more like a bright sun
buried in the dark.
                    And how we digressed
in this chaste mash up of he to she, scarcely
undressed, all those buttons and zips, quaking lips,
and never mind whose hair or what infinite
                    care, one or the other
recalling a stutter in childhood
                    and the nimbleness required
                    in saying, clearly, without laughing:
Peter Piper picked a peck of pickled peppers,
and then mastering, without hint of a lisp:
She sells seashells down by the seashore.
          Our tongue-twisting killed some time,
along with our pristine holding of hands (okay, so maybe
                            you weren't really sitting on me
          and the car wasn't even French
but a Honda—still, a metallic blue, and small,
      so that we were pressed together,
our touted bodies preparing
                    for later tricks of memory, and we never
really did get to any sweet commotion or
more flagrant kisses than the one you left
                    like a gentle burr on the side of my mouth,
          which was slightly parted, true,
and expectant, that's also right,
          admitting to the risk
      under my skin, and yours, of belonging
to no one in particular)—
                    at that moment, we still remained free
to be claimed by the horse, unbridled,

carried away with cadence,
a few nonsensical sounds tripping from our mouths
   in the mad rush of falling light along the shore,
we still belonged to no one in particular
       (have I already said that?)
and yes, you probably recall
some of our trotted-out words of derring-do, like *frisson*
or *farouche*
     sounding foreign between us
(but hey, this is Canada, and some of us speak French
         only grudgingly, as last resort)
   or thought our hands cleaving
beneath the pulled-up sweaters, *pat-a-cake, pat-a-cake, baker's man,*
bake me a cake as fast as you can,
pat it, and prick it— and mark it with b,
  and put it in the oven
      for baby and me
far too likely
    to end in "recrimination after fornication"
    (your quaint rhyme, not mine), you falling
strangely silent
      while I pandered, *tant pis*, to your sudden mood;
   you no doubt still believe
we were in bucket seats a thousand miles apart,
diligent
   in slamming the barn door (it was red,
heavy and red) after the horse had already escaped:
(we could hear its astonished gallop along the beach, charging
into the rollers, *chevaucher le ressac*)
     and we talked, all night it seemed,
of that silly horse, how fraught
   in its freedom, how light on its feet
in delivering us from slippery translation,
       one to another.
Yes, and wasn't our act of gentling
the horse, coaxing it, with its heaving flanks and startled eyes,
to come along
   finally a question? *Chevaucheras—*
tu avec moi?
     Will you ride with me?

Naming the Intended

I.

       ghost words,
an odd crew of miscreant sounds
      and misprints by nineteenth-century scribes
 appearing in dictionaries, but never actually used—
      like *kime* or *morse*
for the intended words *knife* and *nurse*—
open our minds to what's possible;
even those names once nailed down
           in a particular place, by want,
arrive haphazardly in our mouths
as ghosted echoes, may be German
      or Cree, like the paint-blistered signs
of faded welcome: *Willkommen*
become simply *Will...* or... *ommen*
in the blown-down towns as you pass
         through, like a hole in a sweater
and you the bee, wanting things
from the inside out,
      words opening
the forlorn sash on a window
the way the farmer has always said it
to his father, *Schiebefenster,*
the double-hung casement nearly extinct,
      the light in the mullions
once framed by wood grown in stands of white birch: *sakaw*
as the early people round Battleford
might have said, slim forests
splintered into dark, autumn branches,
      the air *kimed*
by the sharp scent of the prairie's burning-off,
its steeled hue
        as we *morse* thoughts of winter,
the snow geese overhead trailing their haunt sounds
for summer's falling down

II.

    words may need other words
                to persuade us
  fast green
            (a green dye that stains plant tissues)
we startle, open our eyes wide
when peering through microscopes,
the squiggle of imperceptible worlds made plain,
amused that *fast*
      and *green,* apart
mean no such thing

             or *false fruit*
a strawberry comes to mind: of the rose family,
its red flesh the flower's receptacle,
    the true fruits being the small prickly pips,
this fact astonishing,
    that we are tasting the sweetness of something real
and something only seeming to be,
    its delicate, wild solace once a medieval sign of purity—
there wasn't much science then, only belief—
    so we take bites
           of the heart-shaped pretender,
           doubting perfection

III.

    how about *Bruno*
small town in Saskatchewan
with a name like a fetching dog, sturdy
and reliable,
       you assume
it could be any old town with a church
plunked down on the prairie—
a nuts-and-bolts sanity, an everydayness of hard labour
    but there's a fleetness here, a heady tending
toward *otherness*—
       the name belonging to a saint

whose feast day is today, a Carthusian,
      professor of miracles
at Rheims, said to have brought great wrongs to light,
who retreated later to Calabria,
kept cattle and few companions, spent years
in an aching translation of the Psalter, "Jubilate Deo,"
a quiet shout-out to God,
               so that he might be heard

there are ranging herds, still,
      a handful of farmers in their raised dust:
note the baseball diamond overgrown with sage
      then follow the path to the graves,
those names within a town's calling
            (population 601, give or take)
the Ursuline motherhouse
      once here, discreet, at some remove
from the Benedictine abbey down the road
where the Elizabethan nuns, in their heavy habits, answered the call
to nurse the local farmers and fruitful mothers,
      hung white sheets out to dry in the prairie winds
and worked long hours in preserving the vast gardens
      for the priests and Brothers, bearing the bushels
of apple and damson plum, gleaning
the last turnips and potatoes, and never minding
(or so it is said) they had no children
to speak of;
           these ceded women
in their peaked hats, hustling to the urgent ringing
            of bells, living as long as their prayers
provided (save those struck by the Spanish flu),
their resilience attributed
      to a clever hiding of the *hippocampus,*
the right side of the brain: *two ridges, highly*
developed in primates and whales… in expression
of responses, in emotion,
such as anger

                 or fear

IV.

     only one remains
of these spare, apportioning women,
a hermit, who lives apart—
         remembered as *Suzanne*
(bringing to mind love and oranges,
the Cohenesque chant,
           our being taken
all too willing, to the river's edge);

          she is old now, fading
among the white-stalked forests of paper birch,
her last tasking a frail one,
         the study of *feathers*:
the body covering of birds'
outgrowths, a composing of keratin
providing heat—
         giving the grounded body
a streamlined shape, those feathers
at the wings and tail
           the barest essentials for flight—

Sound & Belonging

"That's when the voice from the galaxy
comes back saying, praise be, it had a good
sleep; it is ready to translate."
                    —"From Outer Space," Ruth Stone

I.   Sound

ears are eclectic: poking out
as afterthought to a face, your satellite-dish curlicues
                    pick and choose
among the headlong and humdrum, cupping
each delicate strand of sound's escape
if only to find the single struck note
                              that doesn't belong—
        small snicker of fire, scuff of footstep, might be
a mouse in the kitchen cupboard or crumbling plaster
            warning of seismic shift two hundred miles south,
the old bricked storefronts by the harbour in Seattle
                    toppled—you hear the fracture's
crisp note of surprise long before
            you see the ruin on the news

a music box stored in your ear's attic
it dances with memory, do-si-do, swing your lost partner—
you're always revisiting an old Sting tune,
the laid-down lovers in the barley
            or the soft-plucked sound of his kissing you, the man you adore,
        there, by your right ear, the sweet upset
of his tender attention when you tend to forget
            your own ticklish ears, gazing instead
into grand canyons or beguiling eyes,
                blabbermouths always stealing the show

you can shake your head in disbelief

sweep your daft, labyrinthine devices
  clear of acoustic debris in foreign cities,
the sounds raw and alarming, you can't make out
what they mean (the reaping of lavender
  drove Van Gogh crazy, that shuck-shucking
as darkness fell to lilac)
        yet ears are true adepts,
always on the case, discreet Dada detectives
perfect vessels for whistle-blowers
  picking up on nuance
of infamy or insult, the small gasps of the secretly well loved
  as prelude to betrayal—
all you meant, or might yet do better
        coming to rest
  in the shy coves of your ears

ears have the last laugh
  (or at least hear it)
the doctor on his final rounds
coming to see how you were keeping
  and you weren't
able to say, I'm stuck here between worlds
soon passing to nought
  or else fields of gold

you're on audio-pilot, tuned in
  to what transpired in the end—
the small popping sound of skyward travel
  and what might still
chisel its way into sound above the world's distant hum—
  what you hear is what you ride with
     toward high-strung paradise

the nurses tidying up, laying your hands just so
  closing your stymied eyes
and saying, she's gone, there was no suffering—
she wants "Bohemian Rhapsody" at her wake,

the Queen version, imagine!
and laughing—
            you hear the peals of joy
like small, struck bells
inside huge, rustling human bodies
they are glad it went well, this whole death business
they are pitter-pattering
            like the first hushed touches
            of an early summer's rain on each new tree's new leaf

II.   Belonging

if time was long for a long time, now
            time's tether is short, frayed—
searing and tight, and you struggle against it,
                                    afraid for release

it was long for a long time
and now time reminds you to make it snappy;
            you loosen its clocked grip
only in your sleep, where dreams, like envious
                                    experiments in science or love
prove a slippery osmosis, the stronger
solutions calling toward the weaker, swilling
in circles, you swimming with acrobats and flying with fish
            and if the circus of childhood and all dreaming
was once slowly unspooling, and endless,
                        now time is short
two shakes
            the quick-quick flicking of a lamb's tail
                        as measure, of instance (and innocence)
by the makers of the atom bomb—10 implausible
nanoseconds of countdown—
                        quick-quick, you're running out of time
            trying to remember a word,
the way it surprised you, caught you
off guard when you were entitled, still, to a long time

and you don't know
where you might have dropped the sound
        from your mouth's careless red pocket
when you were still young, parsing
in pristine white gloves at the Redwood Athenaeum
the tick-tock broken-clock scribbles
                of Emily Dickinson, who was afraid—
and unafraid to say so—of sharp gossip and fast trains,
        and you look for the bold or delicate
word in the dead grass before the house of Henry James
under the spreading chestnut, as if you had lost
        house keys or a very, very small dog or husband,
and you look over the edge of the world
where you once travelled in the red dust Down Under,
sat among the mother-clans who thought your sun-streaked hair
        and childish air of surprise
a likeness to Marilyn Monroe—how you all howled with laughter—
their teasing in muddled pidgin,
                        fierce in its sputter
as they tried on their finery of hand-me-down clothes
from the compassionate white cities,
                                these story-tell women
protesting how they had lost the old chatter
        for the long-walking to water among the ghost gums,
could no longer sing out their own word of mouth,
once peppered with seven hundred forms
                of naming slipped time—

        or you might have abandoned
the word on a different continent, closer to home
the land flat, reverberating,
        stretched taut like a beaten drum top at summer's end,
tractors and trains grinding their percussive lines
into the prairie's worry-song of harvest,
        and you looking for missed paths, the untouched
leaves, twigs, grasses that have no choice
                        but to grow, before dying—
you lifted above

90

a stand of white-barked birch,
your arms casting winged shadows over the plains
                and that's the devil of dreams, how they circle, in tiers
as if life were a wedding cake, and you the uninvited
                guest, taking a bite of sweet reprieve here or there—
but time is short, stuttered, breaking up
like the light among those riffling trees
                in the middle of nowhere, the town so small
you had to hang a sign by the lumberyard saying "Passenger"
to hop the bus to Saskatoon, when you were still young—

                and you can't recall
if the sensation of the sound you once called out
is a cool one, somewhat estranged,
        the cold fire of winter in your fingers and feet burning,
        this trip-trapping of a word
like someone trying to break through tangled brush
                to find another
just by the crackle underfoot of an imagined footstep,
                or whether this sainted password—
the *skaw-skaw-skaw* of prayer when you can't find a soul
                and you're alone, in the dream of passing over—
is blistering hot, full of risk and chase;
        words spin and collide, send up sparks
in the autumn's burning off, dark shapes stooped in the fields
        gleaning the last of the apples and potatoes,
the Brothers of St. Benedict, in their dark vestments, making motions
        toward evening vespers, their chant on your behalf
still wrung out in Latin, as if nothing has changed
                in a thousand years in the fallen world

        the voices, those holding sway
and all the others brought up short, never having been
                        truly heard, are almost gone
and time is sudden, slanted, sharp as pickets
on a broken fence in the long grasses,
                        to trip you up;
and quick-quick, lamb's tail,

                                        you remember the poets,
            huge with sound at St. Pete's, shouting above
                        the clanging of knives and forks in the abbey's dining hall
            the clamour of Ashbery and Berryman, a poem named simply
            "Poem," by Frank O'Hara, and the San Francisco heyday
            of Jack Spicer, his name in itself a bright-sounding feat—
                        you remember
            the line *of blood and tangerines*, but not who wrote it—
            the language as you knew it, the jazzed-up rants
                        made brave after the world's wars, nothing to lose
            in being off-the-beaten-path beat-poet irreverent,
                                        is falling away
            and maybe your forlorn word
            was borrowed, or stolen
                        and you have to give it back,
                    it's rubbing against you, begging to be heard
            and won't be shaken loose—

                        and then you see him,
            he's been there the whole time, listening in
                        to the writers' ruckus, standing irresolute
            by the milk cooler, not sure where he belongs—
            you're surprised to see him here at all
                        in the dream of your dying, supplicant
            among the raving poets and august Catholics on retreat,
                        as if he could yet
            be granted ancestors and calm—
                        says he's not necessarily Cree
            and you haven't the faintest, don't know
            a switch of braided sweetgrass from a horse's rump, can't say
            you believe in the cleansing of ghosted rooms
                        by way of smoking sage, can't foresee
            how long the First Peoples might yet carry
                                        that dark startle in their eyes;
            but he's willing to share
            a few moot syllables, one-two-three
            his father kept hidden in a dark schooling of rote shame,
                        the children forever lisping excuses

     for rhyming things with home—
he's young, hoping to beat the odds,
reminds you
    how trespass and forgiveness
are close kin, following the same abraded paths
of least resistance—
   "like water," he says, "like the air itself"

then touches your sleeve, says the word
you've forgotten (if you ever knew it),
    its sound like a distant crow's call
among the dark branches of a come winter, the white sleeves
  of snow—sharp-soft, sharp-soft—
shows you what it means, a *brushing up against*
light as a fallen leaf—
     you can scarcely feel his approach—
there's mischief afoot and you didn't see it coming,
and you're starting to understand
    how a quiet rustle and hovering, shiver
of bright autumn trees, any small motion
      toward another
might mean recognition, an entrance—
not only the inkling between lovers, or the lost
    among their gods,
he eases the risk in your mind, assures you
      this teasing out
of closeness can be with a sister, or friend, complete stranger
    as comfort or courage,
he's had something precious lifted from him, is offering a gift—
takes his own sweet time, as if time were long again,
    repeats the sound one, two, three
like a small homecoming in his mouth
     and you try and try
to spit out the long-forgotten soft-sharp word
like a child's first taw-dee-dah,
   how we celebrate that first gawp of amaze,
make up tender or fantastic stories so we won't lose
   the chastened sigh of summer gone, a once-latitude

and flown praise—
the word's sound rising with the hot-watchful sun
           and falling with the crow's comic rebuke
       summer's-skaw, summer's-skaw
and you've almost fastened the feeling down, soft-sharp at its edges,
your heart's drumming like the scorched prairie in its thirst—
you are hurtling into the dark,
                touching everyone in your passing,
the poets brushing by, leaning on one another, softly
                                and laughing—
because time is short, and time recalls
old wounds of flight and unbelonging, traces their relief,
and then time is ever so long, follows
                   the fine white lines of healing, like shooting stars—
the bright trailings
            of lives you might have once missed

Correspondence: Three Slips of the Tongue

I.

"I remember now, it was in the Fowley book."

She had started combining words. Her memory otherwise tickety-boo: my aunt could recall the exact page in the Cowley-Faulkner correspondence. The old fabulist, Faulkner, remarking that a Warner's movie-type was making ten times the money he did as scriptwriter. Just for inventing a screen gesture, Bogart tossing a book of matches to Bacall to suggest he thought her useful for lighting up. A *tramp*, as Faulkner puts it.

So, a slip of the tongue perhaps. *Lapsus linguae.* A wrong-headed blurt that might distance lovers, start wars—it was no fun being misunderstood.

"You mean Faulkner's letters to his editor, Malcolm Cowley?"

"The Fowley book," she repeated, her face pained, knowing the sound to be false.

The brain is a complicated stricture, clocking along, and just one little glitch the whole thing gone haywire. Did I say *stricture*? I meant *structure*, as in composition, as in synergy. As in *The Sound and the Fury* becoming simply *The Found*.

II.

As a child I rightly believed the words *scripture* and *scripted* related. *Constricted*, with its sinewy, tight sound, seemed a close cousin. I knew by heart the familial feeling of constraint, was often confined to the house as punishment. *Grounded* being a term for shipwreck or downed plane, I'd been taken out of action. And this was war. I felt compelled to carry out reconnaissance. Watch my back and regroup. Make a daring escape. High stakes were being played out; I hadn't signed up for anything but love. I knew by uneasy hearsay a flight to Algiers or Cairo could be stuck on the tarmac, the leverage of taking hostages. Because they were loved—by someone, somewhere, that was the sticking point. The outrage later on behalf of the fallen, the question of who might have been spared. Paradise was often overbooked.

Words can be salutation, truce; the Faulkner letters mention a *shotgun bungalow*, a narrow pitch of rooms scarcely as wide as two men laid end to end. In a southern story the lowered bodies were typically black, and struggling to rise. A shot from the front porch could neatly exit by the back stoop. I was reminded of our spare privacies, and how cleanly the crow flies. A word used before I was born, by a crack storyteller, flew through me and landed. Without meaning to, I stepped into a darkened bedroom, heard a shotgun blast, and slipped out the back.

III.

Thoughts of loosened slaves, and blame, led to my reading Harper Lee's *Mockingbird* story aloud to my aunt. She was on "tenterbooks," she said, as Boo Radley placed his treasures for the children in a hollowed tree. With her tripped-up tongue, she was relearning innocence, all the meanings uncertain.

British writer, William Trevor, admitted he often wrote of women because he wasn't one. We are most curious about being born and dying, E.M. Forster said, when there are no words. Hence the latest craze, a *living wake* for those enduring a dead-end disease. Laughter is key: the poked fun and spilled praise helps us pass over, in good spirits. So says a ha-ha therapist who studies the brain's affinity for the absurd or incongruous. A child of four laughs four hundred times a day, while the ho-hum adult gives only a dozen grudging guffaws. Dr. Mirth suggests we stir the pot, grief with joy, the more hee-haws the better. Which brings us back to scripture and a so-called good life, what we are conscripted to do, until the end, the dying invited as honoured guests.

"Like children, we defy all warning and explanation, want to see a thing for ourselves," my aunt said, gloriously on her game in that moment.

Paradise, Later Years

I.

       I am popular with animals:
they approach the kitchen at dawn, in cahoots,
one already caterwauling for hours,
the large black dogs prostrating themselves at my feet
in ridiculous mime of hunt-and-gather, the pup sitting cleverly
kitty-corner to the fridge she admires for its cool aspects
of foraging,
             and the whole lot fix their eyes
on the particular way I lift my buttered pumpernickel toast,
whether I am feeling in good spirits, or not;
we have rules, of course,
         I am the shilly-shallying boss
and they win only fallen morsels or mouldy bits of cheese
according to age or appetite,
              and bear me little grudge
for rearing up out of bed and living in people years,
     a seemingly grand stretch of time
from where my passel sit, kowtowing—

but in truth, we squander most of it, rage inwardly, lie
blithely to loved ones, betray already feint
        loyalties, and worry
(but not enough, never enough) about consuming
     free-range eggs (the happier sort)
or bacon rind being not so far removed from the sordid
circumstances of factory pork, and why we didn't know for so long
that lobster, in a quite unlimited way, *do* suffer,
don't even go into shock when they're boiled alive, every nerve
ending on the job, and people still not minding;

       I scarcely believe any longer
in a scurrilous god having once granted me, or anyone else,
dominion over even a fishbowl—

all that remains at the tail end, I tell
my riff-raff crew of moochers, is to renege
            or chafe in some pukingly stale hospital room,
                        everything we've been given
narrowed to impasse, hardened,
like our hapless arteries, the sorry
                        constraint of our hearts—

    the animals, *my* animals
clearly unmoved by this human horror show
in which they repeat themselves in faux handshakes
and pretend fetch, wag and loll, *play dead*,
make cavalier forays with unbidden enthusiasm
onto verboten sofas or dining tables, really ham it up,
            as if they'll stoop to anything
foolish, and thereby more endearing,
that might win me over—
                        I've taught them everything I know:

that greed is largely forgivable
grandstanding, and making a small ruckus is good, might still
                        change the world, and thirst
when it hits you, despite an abundance of water and wine
for some, and nothing dripping down the spout for all the rest,
is merely stoppered-up desire,
            and what makes humans so different
from that lobster not going at all gently
is that we can have what we want—
                        scary thought.

    Nights, the animals' unslippered feet
dream in slant jigs of slim escapes from the benign
confines of armchairs and cheesy pet-designer duvets;
            they rise in mid-nap to prowl, make jungle noises,
bark idiotically at shadows as if there might be
real intruders, their hackles stiff with nostalgia
            while ghosts enter the premises—

the bachelor farmer who once lived here
hung his trousers and his pans, both, on one spike
in the fir cladding of the summer porch, and might well
                have thought to hang himself
from a rafter, what with a fire razing the place to the ground
and his one true love
                killed by some fluking logs in her father's mill.
So he arrives, still bearing clumsy bouquets
plucked from the neighbour's wisteria in 1919,
circumspect coyotes passing the house without a single yip,
barred owls elegantly performing their killing
in the nearby forest, and lately, even though they're supposed to be
                holed up, there's a hint of bear scat
in the dark, loosened air:
                and so it goes, each night, a revelry.

"Lie down," I growl, "go back to sleep."
But my beasts in suburban recline are busy, very busy;
                they chitter and yowl, curse softly
like children's voices in distant rooms, hoping yet
                to inherit what is rightly theirs,
something more gorse green and higgledy-piggledy
than the surrounding close-cropped lawns glimpsed
from sealed windows, the way the abandoned summer furniture,
knee deep in mounds of shucked leaves, and lately bright
against the dark with buttressed snow,
                                startles them, each time;

they should get a load of what I'm conjuring—
witless spoofs like daytime television unspooling,
even the subconscious these days
an advertising ploy,
        all the malls replete with perfect strangers
always love-shopping, and bearing their brand new devices
for hairless *that* or sunny *there*—
                sometimes I *awaken*, but not quite,
like a woman in the first pages of old novels

when she suddenly realizes
with a candle's flaming against a slight breeze from a window
that she's at some exact turning point
                in an auspicious century, and despite
a generous endowment from some hoary uncle
and a languorous mill on her very own splish-sploshing floss,
she is still unmarried—
                I generally cut the dream off then,
stark naked and struck with the kind of fear
that permeates joy,
                                    starts to ruin everything.

Meanwhile my plucky animals
                        are soothing their own distempers—
slather themselves in ancient swamps or scamper
with creatures long extinct on the shimmering savannah—
they travel the distance in visceral, hard-wired fashion,
            don't need deals on a ticket south
            and look good to themselves in each escapade
if only they are brave,
                that's all that's required
on a rocky ledge in the Andalusians, or sniffing the wind
on picture-perfect buttes in Montana, a magnificent storm
hulking on the brow of the horizon
                                with enough electric commotion
in the brouhaha clouds to send my fantastic superhero house pets
            scampering through the blown grasses—

            When we shamble toward
our piecemeal sharing of foodstuffs, mornings,
            are these ancient heroics still what they want?

II.

> What do I know—
> > I've only seen wild horses once,
> set against a blue light high up in shale canyons
> in the Pryor Mountains;
> > > I was still young,
> heady with searching for something my father had promised
> > would be remarkable,
> and then the mustangs stared us down,
> a small grouping, their feathered legs half in shadow,
> > > and the way they took flight—
> *upwards*, it seemed, through the radiant, shaken dust—
> > > > well, I was blinded, thought them angels.

> > Having been found, they were clearly afraid—
> > > and so were we—
> the way my father packed up the camera in a hurry,
> shooed his own small herd of stragglers back toward the car
> > > and drove along the Yellowstone with a vengeance,
> as though his family had prevented him from becoming
> bolder, a sudden cowboy or trick photographer
> > > > capturing the rare moment
> with a rope or a lens,
> > > holding everything in its place,
> an early snow falling in the higher passes, the autumn hills
> staggered with antelope, and twelve signs in total
> of roadside motels called The Sportsman;
> > > > I could see
> how it would be a struggle to stay alive
> > > and look beautiful doing it
> in the way my mother sat proudly in the passenger seat,
> > > > said little all the way home.

III.

I admire the horses, *my* hay-burners,
the ones I keep pent-up on a single hectare
of mostly spent grasses, for still having a clue;
        at each shifting of light
they are newly amazed
by what's changed in the scene while they weren't looking,
a pop can glinting within a greater sea of frost
or man's hat bobbing along the road's verge
        a possible horse tragedy—
they *know* and *know*, like some sort of horse mantra,
they can't afford to fall or be broken,
lose one another in haste,
        and there's strange comfort
for my threesome in pushing through each day's flickering
slide show of strained sun, and showing off
their grandiose caution:
        if they swing around in real alarm
and I just happen to be standing beside the gate,
        lost in thought about an ex-lover, well,
they get me up on my toes, literally
    save my life
and the words *trampled*, or *unaware*,
heart in a million pieces
        become as acute as falling stars.

I once tried to justify keeping horses
as good investments for would-be backyard Olympics
or pending farm taxes, but these days
I confess I sequester them for
        the sake of outrageous beauty—

and we all feel the risk, believe me;
I give them long commutes where I might never return—
        their sorrowful eyes accuse me of this—
and anxious training sessions, in circles, at canters
with horse necks bending just so, at a proper learned cadence,
and between times trick them with a rip-roaring view

to everywhere else but where they're staidly corralled,
restrained from running too hard or too far
just for the nostalgic effect—

      and they can hear the baying of domestic dogs
run amuck as wolves, while I offer them gratuitous hay
      amid an all-they-can-eat buffet
of assorted thistles, dandelion, fescue and orchard grasses
(a few toxic buttercups and ragwort thrown into the mix),
      grant them sweaty flanks
in summer stamping against the bugs, it must be hell,
and cold rusings of rain, westerly winds galore;

      I do the whole moot-horse mock-up
of the way it's always been,
lend their heave-ho retirement under a scant lean-to
some depth and breadth,
      so they can thrill to the nearly wild notion
they might yet come and go
                  as they please;

he formerly a stallion, she still a persnickety she,
the youngster a handsome failure
at the races, one of those ne'er-do-well sons of a good family
inclined to hedging their bets and still losing,
pumping up their spirits with rarified addictions.
The veteran nags were astute in their time at playing polo,
actually bore down on the white zigzag ball
      as if it mattered,
shoulder-checking their rivals at full gallop
so a few men with time on their hands, mostly doctors
      or mobsters swinging mallets,
might feel at the top of their game, really alive—

      My pretty little herd
is impatient for its return to grace;

if, at one time, they were micromanaged
by young girls braiding their unruly forelocks, wanting
to assuage half-ton rebels between their thighs,
that's all over now—

I like swift animals, in huge format,
a hundred feet of intestine neatly tucked into hefty loins:
I'm always shovelling their sweet crap
toward the late summer's nasturtiums blooming nicely
into November and the ripe red tomatoes
        tasting real for a change;
the old shit clings to the new and prolific
in the same stubborn way that the horses, *my* horses,
remain in sight and footloose, both sturdy
and ephemeral,
                bring with them each spring
the lively chit-chat of the swallows newly returned from Bolivia
choosing my sway-backed barn for their thorny bit of child-rearing,
all the nests finally too small, the teetering fledglings
leaving home at a moment's notice—
                the shirkers and shy ones never do well.
Each time it's the same, I delicately
pitchfork the tiny, free-fallen forms into the manure,
hectic parents grieving in swallow trajectory,
        the flies angrily riding horseback,
                        ready to take death far afield.

IV.

        The whole thing's a sham, I'll admit,
I give the animals, *my* animals, mostly circus:
three ring, high-wire, Big Top, cotton candy, fat freakish lady,
Step right up! Step right up! Bring the kids!
Treat yourself to flim-flam spectacle—
quivering snakes and tattoos, cute monkeys with accordions
screeching to calliope refrains,
                and a small harlequin-ruffled dog
with a haunted face riding the shoulders of an equally moribund

clown, his painted tear-dropped face
aghast when the poor pooch is shot from a cannon
                                        to madcap applause—
and let's not forget Sparkly Girl—that's me!—
                    still hot-to-trot in a spangled skirt
astride the grey rump of a stalwart horse moving round and round
in the sawdust: we all earn our keep
                            being somewhat magical.

And that's why the seventeen-year-old tabby
            who's top tiger in my tawdry road show
briefly mauls his keeper and makes his virtual escape,
                    climbs a silver banister to nowhere,
swings without safety net in what seems to him a tingly night sky
and falls mightily
                    down the cellar stairs on Good Friday:
I'm worried, of course I am,
the old kitty's my password at the bank,
                        connects me with the mysteries
of increasing debt (it unnerves me each time the teller
asks me to say M-A-T-T-Y aloud for security reasons);
and any attending vet is bound to charge double
            on a crucifixion holiday just to check out
the poor beast's vestibular function,
tell me his fourth lumbar vertebra isn't any great shakes,
there'll be no more jumping on a hot stove
                    as if through wondrous rings of fire,
and he'll probably suffer
                    another stroke, and I have to *decide*—
now that the cat is mostly addled, walks crab-wise,
has lost his Chicago-blues, hard-smokin' meow,
his modus operandi of complaint, opens his stale mouth
                to no sound at all—

but I read his lips, how he still feels
        like a thirty-something-year-old (in people years)
and I know exactly what he means—

hell, it's no fun calling the shots,
so I grab the limp cat (who literally can't hurt a flea,
he's one step removed from pure metaphor),
                    we made a pact ages ago
when I found the abandoned bobcat look-alike
mewling under a neighbour's hot tub,
            and now the whole death-defying shtick
is right in our faces, it's all we can do
to watch spurious episodes of *Matlock* on somnolent afternoons,
simply sit back and peruse the world with rabbit-ear antennae
pointing east and south,
                        as if to our own personal meccas;

Family Feud is next, I murmur to no one in particular,
                    and he winks one golden eye, as if to say,
Can it get any better than this
in our flickering   K-k-k-kingdom?

V.

        I am comfortable with animals.
So was Emily Carr, and so, too
cantankerous Pound, and Forster,
always finagling his fine prose with constrained servants
and pent-up sexual mores. Rilke not so much.
                    The hairs from the Russian wolfhounds
always posing beside the countess disturbed him,
given his disposition for wearing dark, worsted coats. The noise
            the brutes made when eating.
He had a thing, though, about watching
the pacing of the caged, black panther
in Le Jardin des Plantes in Paris, thought of his mother's
            white hands on the piano
being scarfed by those slavering jaws in captivity,
and felt faint, almost more relieved than ashamed,
studied this auspicious conflict of emotions
        in broken gestalts of old houses and young girls
as only a gifted introvert can.

I once translated the zoo poem
at school, changed the German for *glance*
to the English for *recognition*, took liberties as well
with the morose phrasing for *ceases to be*
                and called it what it was,
a small death of living
within cramped quarters, and we the humdrum caretakers,
            clearly lacking in imagination
to keep and keep and keep our dangerous cobras and cassowaries
at bay, stirring without respite in anticipation
of release;
                in my concocted verse
I opened all the latches in all the wrought-iron gardens
and let the big cat go free—

        for which springing of gates and astonishing
effects (the poem became more a Wallace Stevens affair then,
too modern with chasing foot-policemen and ice cream vendors)
            I was admonished:
my teacher, with his long, brave hair and paisley shirts
                was right to remind me
the poem was more about the person watching
than the pivoting beast behind bars—

                    But is it love
to observe suffering, even grant it
a strained beauty all the better
                    to scribe its effects?
That seemed more like science to me, or law,
                the way you can argue almost anything,
or war, a cruel or ludicrous
end to things before they even begin
than any plain art, and I said so:
                    Isn't the whole point

        to get over ourselves?

VI.

I am lugubrious with animals,
have a certain notoriety for speaking my mind.

Eventually we are all alone,
                    I told the black bear
roosting in my plum tree last summer.
He'd fallen asleep in the upper branches
nicely pruned with his four-hundred-pound butt, *crack-snap!*
and his grizzled muzzle—so a grandpa then
                    and I should show some respect—
peeked through the purpled leaves in my direction
when I tooted the old Chevy's horn, *Boop-hoop, blam, blam!*

                    I had to clear a passage,
get from here to there without dying, without
unduly disturbing him either (it was a real trade-off).
"Get out of my tree, you bad ass,
                    you fruit thug, you big, beautiful bamboozler!" I heckled,
as if he were the last in a series of unrequited loves.
                    "I don't want you here when I get home!"

Profoundly abashed at my blaring use of language
and truck cacophony—
                    or perhaps pretending—
he made no move to clamber down, was not even
furious with himself for overeating.
I envied him that, hadn't meant to insult him—
                    merely rouse him
from some dream of humans as lunch-box providers,
restoring a right-minded hierarchy
to the ancient stature of trees, and all guilty circumstance
                    fractured within my own backyard.
                    I was a god once,

I told him more quietly,
within a breathless sort of cha-cha-cha

rising through the dark limbs of the air—
and it's true, he seemed surprised,
began scratching his left ear—
  I was once round-and-round, and laughing,
shot with quizzical light
     and danced, like Rumi's ecstatic friend,
Shams, who could, by all reports,
feed off the glance of another for a thousand years—

        and will be again.

Notes

Opening Epigraphs:

"The Room." In *When One Has Lived A Long Time Alone,* p44. Galway Kinnell. (New York: Alfred A. Knopf, 1990).

"Tell the Ones You Love." In *Heart Residence: Collected Poems 1967–2017,* p288, Dennis Lee. (Toronto: House of Anansi, 2017).

Notes on the Text:

Epigraph in "Women in December," from "What Were They Like?," in *Poems 1960–1967,* p234, Denise Levertov. (New York: New Directions, 1983).

In the poem "The Odds:" the quote is from "Vertumnus," in *So Forth,* p36–47, Joseph Brodsky. (New York: The Noonday Press, 1996).

In the poem "Yesterday, I looked inside," the quotes refer to the well-known John Donne phrase, "Death, be not proud," and are taken from: Raymond Carver, "Gravy," *A New Path to the Waterfall,* p118. (New York: Atlantic Monthly Press, 1989).

In the poem "*Et alors?*," the French words are purposely playful and distorted, not altogether accurate.

In the poem "Naming the Intended," the Cree word *sakaw* was relayed by a First Nations visitor to the Sage Hill writing colony at St. Peter's College, Muenster, Saskatchewan, and appears in: *Stories of the House People,* Peter Vandall, Joe Douquette (authors), Freda Ahenakew (editor). (Winnipeg: University of Manitoba Press, 1987).

Epigraph in "Sound & Belonging" from "Outer Space," in *In the Dark,* p38 Ruth Stone. (Port Townsend: Copper Canyon Press, 2007).

In the poem "Sound & Belonging," there is intended echo of a Cree word relayed by a First Nations speaker at the Sage Hill writing colony, St. Peter's College, and intended apology for "lost words" in the mother tongues of those First Nations children attending Canada's residential schools.

In the prose poem "Correspondence: Three Slips of the Tongue," the book referred to is *The Faulkner-Cowley File: Letters and Memories, 1944–1962*, Malcolm Cowley. (London: Chatto & Windus, 1966).

Previously Published Poems and Awards

Poems published previously, sometimes in altered versions, appeared in the following literary journals or anthologies, or online.

"Long Weekend," *Vintage 97–98*, p164–165, League of Canadian Poets. (Kingston: Quarry Press, 1998).

"Which One of Us, in White," in *Down in the Valley: Contemporary Writing of the Fraser Valley,* , p20, ed. Trevor Carolan (Victoria: Ekstasis Editions, 2004).

"Yesterday, I Looked Inside" was shortlisted for the CBC Poetry Prize, winning the People's Choice Award, 2012, published online.

"Paradise, Later Years" was the co-winner of *The Malahat Review*'s Long Poem Prize, 2009, and the subsequent winner of a National Magazine Award, Gold, 2010.

Acknowledgments

So many long poems and so little time: I have to thank those who recognized the struggle and gave me the reassurance, dinners, hay for my horses and, yes, even money in hard times to help words take shape. You granted me precious time and also that other thing called "permission," to go ahead, make my voice heard.

I would like to express my gratitude for the support of the late Bud Allison, who encouraged my early writing, and to my mentors, Tim Lilburn, Andreas Schroeder, Patrick Friesen and the late Galway Kinnell, who all said the same thing in different ways: be bold in imagining, careful in craft. I owe a debt to the friends and colleagues who read and thought deeply, laughed hard: Heidi Greco, Sharon Brown, Hal Wake, Miranda Hill, Genni Gunn and Frank Hook, and thanks as well to Larry and Karola Stinson, Phyllis Surges, Helen Tervo, Joe Baker and Alan and Kirsten Rawkins, whose kindness and patience cleared the way. Elina Taillon and Dr. Shannon MacLean granted me insights into "listening," Kat Wahamaa gave me creative opportunity and Dr. Ken Macquisten has long shared his respect for animal smarts/angst. I am forever grateful for the support of the late Ann and Lyman Henderson for their love of the arts as sustenance for life, pure and simple.

And it gives me great joy to thank my daughter, Alexis, for her questions of how to bear water, wear feathers!

A big hometown parade of thanks to Vici Johnstone, of Caitlin Press, for her belief in my poems, that they would be considered deserving of brave new readers! And to my editors, Yvonne Blomer and Holly Vestad, thank you both for dancing with my words so lightly.